GOLANG PROGRAMMING FOR BEGINNERS

A Step-by-Step Guide to Learning Go for Modern Software Development

KRISTINE ELLIS

Chapter 1: Introduction to Golang

1.1 Why Learn Go?

Programming languages shape how developers write code, build applications, and solve problems. With so many languages available, choosing the right one depends on performance needs, ease of learning, scalability, and long-term relevance. **Go (or Golang)** is a language that checks all these boxes, making it a preferred choice for modern software development.

1.1.1 The Growing Popularity of Go

Go has gained widespread adoption across industries, particularly in cloud computing, microservices, and high-performance applications. Created by Google and backed by a strong open-source community, it is used by companies like Uber, Dropbox, Netflix, and Kubernetes. Its simplicity, speed, and efficiency make it an excellent choice for both startups and large-scale enterprise applications.

1.1.2 Simplicity and Readability

One of Go's biggest strengths is its **simple and clean syntax**. Unlike languages with complex class hierarchies, Go enforces a minimalist approach, making it **easy to learn** even for beginners. Its **concise** and **consistent** syntax reduces unnecessary complexity, allowing developers to focus on writing efficient code rather than dealing with boilerplate or excessive configurations.

1.1.3 High Performance with a Compiled Language

Go is a **statically typed, compiled language**, meaning it translates code into machine instructions before execution. This results in **blazing-fast performance**, often outperforming interpreted languages like Python and JavaScript. Since Go compiles directly into a single binary executable, it avoids runtime dependencies, making deployment seamless and efficient.

1.1.4 Built-In Concurrency Support

Concurrency—the ability to run multiple tasks simultaneously—is crucial for modern applications. Go has **first-class concurrency support** through **goroutines and channels**, making it easier to build highly concurrent applications compared to traditional threading models in Java or Python. Goroutines are lightweight and execute independently, allowing Go programs to handle thousands or even millions of concurrent tasks efficiently.

1.1.5 Efficient Memory Management

Unlike languages that require manual memory management (e.g., C, C++), Go includes **garbage collection**, automatically freeing unused memory. However, Go's garbage collector is designed for high efficiency, ensuring low latency and minimal impact on application performance. This makes Go a great choice for **real-time systems and scalable applications**.

1.1.6 Cross-Platform Compilation

Go allows developers to **compile programs for multiple platforms** (Windows, Linux, macOS, etc.) from a single codebase. With Go's built-in cross-compilation features, developers can build binaries for different operating systems without requiring external tools, making it an ideal choice for **distributed systems and cloud applications**.

1.1.7 Strong Standard Library

Go includes a **rich standard library** with built-in support for networking, file handling, JSON parsing, cryptography, and more. Developers can accomplish a lot without relying on third-party libraries, ensuring **secure and stable applications** with fewer dependencies.

1.1.8 Go is Designed for the Cloud

Cloud-native applications demand lightweight, efficient, and scalable languages. Go was built with cloud computing in mind, making it a **top choice for Kubernetes, Docker, and other cloud-native technologies**. Many cloud infrastructure tools and microservices frameworks are written in Go due to its speed and scalability.

1.1.9 Growing Job Market and Career Opportunities

The increasing adoption of Go means that **demand for Go developers is on the rise**. Companies looking to build scalable and high-performance applications actively seek Go expertise. Whether it's in **backend development, DevOps, microservices, or cloud platforms**, knowing Go opens doors to lucrative career opportunities.

1.1.10 Go is Open Source and Has a Strong Community

Go is fully open source and actively maintained by Google and a **large community of contributors**. This means it continuously evolves with improvements, bug fixes, and feature updates. Developers also have access to numerous **learning resources, open-source libraries, and frameworks**, making it easier to get started and grow in the Go ecosystem.

1.2 History and Purpose of Go

Go's origin story is rooted in the challenges faced by Google's engineers. In the mid-2000s, Google's massive infrastructure relied on languages like C++, Java, and Python, each with its own **performance trade-offs** and **complexity issues**. The need for a language that combined the **efficiency of C, the simplicity of Python, and the concurrency support of Java** led to the creation of Go.

1.2.1 The Birth of Go

In 2007, three prominent Google engineers—**Robert Griesemer, Rob Pike, and Ken Thompson**—began working on a new language that would solve **scalability and development speed issues** within Google's infrastructure. They aimed to create a language that was:

✔ **Fast** like C/C++
✔ **Simple** like Python
✔ **Safe** with garbage collection
✔ **Efficient** in concurrency handling

By 2009, Go was introduced to the public as an **open-source project**, quickly gaining attention from developers looking for a modern alternative to traditional languages.

1.2.2 What Problems Did Go Solve?

Go was designed to **simplify software development** while maintaining the **power of low-level languages**. The three major problems it aimed to fix were:

1. Performance Issues in High-Scale Systems

Google's infrastructure required languages like Java and Python for development ease, but these languages suffered from performance bottlenecks. C++ was fast but **too complex** for rapid iteration. Go was introduced as a **high-performance alternative with the simplicity of scripting languages**.

2. Slow Compilation Times

Large-scale systems require constant code modifications, but C++ and Java's **slow compilation times** significantly impacted productivity. Go was designed to **compile extremely fast**, reducing developer wait time and increasing efficiency.

3. Concurrency Limitations

Traditional threading models in Java, C, and Python were **resource-heavy and hard to manage**. Go introduced **goroutines**, which are **lightweight threads** that use minimal memory and allow highly concurrent applications without unnecessary overhead.

1.2.3 Key Features That Set Go Apart

After years of refinement, Go was officially released in **2012 (version 1.0)** and introduced several groundbreaking features:

- **Simplicity & Readability** – A clean, minimal syntax makes Go easy to learn.
- **Fast Compilation** – Go compiles quickly, even for large projects.
- **Memory Safety** – Includes garbage collection and automatic memory management.
- **First-Class Concurrency** – Goroutines and channels simplify parallel computing.
- **Static Typing with Dynamic Feel** – While statically typed, Go avoids verbosity.

- **Powerful Standard Library** – Built-in support for networking, cryptography, and more.

1.2.4 Go's Adoption in the Industry

Go's **simplicity, speed, and efficiency** made it a natural fit for **backend services, cloud computing, and DevOps tools**. Some major projects and platforms written in Go include:

- **Docker** – The most widely used containerization platform.
- **Kubernetes** – The industry-standard container orchestration system.
- **Terraform** – A widely used infrastructure-as-code tool.
- **Prometheus** – A powerful monitoring system.
- **Hugo** – A fast static site generator.
- **Uber, Netflix, Dropbox** – Companies that use Go for high-performance backend services.

1.2.5 Why Go Continues to Grow

Go's development is actively managed by **Google and the open-source community**, ensuring constant improvement. The language has evolved **without breaking backward compatibility**, making it stable for long-term use.

With continuous refinements and support for modern software trends like **cloud computing, microservices, and AI**, Go remains **one of the most relevant and in-demand programming languages today**.

Go is a **modern, powerful, and efficient language** built to tackle the challenges of large-scale software development. Whether you are new to programming or an experienced developer looking for a **faster and more scalable** alternative, Go offers the **best of both worlds**—simplicity and performance.

1.3 Go vs. Other Programming Languages (Python, Java, C, JavaScript)

Every programming language has its strengths and trade-offs, and developers choose a language based on factors like performance, ease of learning, ecosystem, and use cases. Go was designed to bridge the gap between the efficiency of low-level languages like C/C++ and the simplicity of high-level languages like **Python**. Let's compare Go with some of the most widely used languages in software development.

1.3.1 Go vs. Python

Python is one of the most popular programming languages, known for its **simplicity and versatility**. It is widely used in web development, data science, machine learning, and automation. However, it has certain limitations when compared to Go.

Feature	Go	Python
Performance	**Much faster** due to static typing and compilation	Slower due to dynamic typing and interpretation
Concurrency	**First-class support** with goroutines	Multi-threading is complex and requires extra libraries (GIL limitation)
Memory Management	Efficient **garbage collection**	Python's garbage collection can cause performance issues
Ease of Learning	Simple but requires understanding of pointers, structs	Extremely beginner-friendly
Use Cases	Cloud computing, networking, system programming	Data science, web development, automation

✔ **When to choose Go?** If you need high performance, concurrency, and scalability for backend services, APIs, and cloud applications.
✔ **When to choose Python?** If you are working on AI, machine learning, automation, or scripting-heavy applications.

1.3.2 Go vs. Java

Java is a **battle-tested** enterprise language used in web applications, backend services, and mobile app development. Go simplifies many of the complexities Java brings, particularly in areas like concurrency and deployment.

Feature	Go	Java
Performance	Faster (compiled directly to machine code)	Slower (JVM adds overhead)
Concurrency	**Goroutines** are lightweight and efficient	Uses **threads**, which are more resource-intensive
Syntax	Minimalist and concise	Verbose with complex class hierarchies
Memory Management	Automatic **garbage collection**	JVM garbage collection (can cause latency)
Deployment	**Single binary executable** (no external dependencies)	Requires JVM runtime

✔

When to choose Go? If you want a lightweight, fast, and modern alternative to Java for backend services and microservices.
✔ **When to choose Java?** If you need a robust ecosystem for large enterprise applications or Android development.

1.3.3 Go vs. C/C++

C and C++ are powerful languages used for **low-level system programming, embedded systems, and game development**. Go was designed to bring **C-like performance** while eliminating complexity.

Feature	Go	C/C++
Performance	Close to C, but slightly slower due to garbage collection	**Faster** since it has no garbage collector
Memory Management	Automatic (garbage collector)	Manual memory allocation required
Ease of Learning	Easier (simplified syntax)	**Steeper learning curve**
Concurrency	**Built-in concurrency**	Uses **manual threading**, which is complex

✔ **When to choose Go?** If you need near-C performance but don't want to deal with manual memory management.

✔ **When to choose C/C++?** If you're developing **high-performance applications** like operating systems, game engines, or embedded systems.

1.3.4 Go vs. JavaScript

JavaScript is the dominant language for **frontend web development** and is also widely used on the backend with Node.js. However, Go is **faster and more efficient** for backend services.

Feature	Go	JavaScript (Node.js)
Performance	Faster (compiled)	Slower (interpreted)
Concurrency	Goroutines for parallel execution	Event-driven model (async/await)
Use Cases	Backend services, APIs, networking	Web development, frontend and backend (full-stack)
Syntax	More structured and strict	Loosely typed, flexible

✔

When to choose Go? If you're building **high-performance backend services** or cloud applications.

✔ **When to choose JavaScript?** If you need full-stack web development with **both frontend and backend in the same language.**

1.4 What You Can Build With Go

Go is known for **speed, concurrency, and efficiency,** making it suitable for a wide range of applications. Here are some of the **most common and powerful use cases**:

1.4.1 Web Applications & APIs

Go is widely used in backend development to create **fast and scalable APIs**. Many frameworks like **Gin, Echo, and Fiber** help developers build web applications efficiently.

* **Examples**: RESTful APIs, GraphQL services, authentication systems.
* **Who Uses It?** Uber, Dropbox, and Medium.

8

1.4.2 Cloud Computing & Microservices

Go is the **backbone of cloud-native technologies**. Many cloud platforms and microservice-based architectures rely on Go for its performance and concurrency.

- **Examples**: Kubernetes (written in Go), serverless applications.
- **Who Uses It?** Google Cloud, Docker, Kubernetes.

1.4.3 System Programming & Networking

Go is an excellent choice for building **high-performance networking tools**, VPNs, and proxy servers due to its **low memory footprint and concurrency model**.

- **Examples**: Load balancers, proxies, DNS servers.
- **Who Uses It?** Cloudflare, Netflix.

1.4.4 DevOps & Automation

Go is a favorite for writing **CLI tools and automation scripts** for DevOps and infrastructure management.

- **Examples**: CI/CD pipelines, monitoring tools, Kubernetes automation.
- **Who Uses It?** Terraform, Prometheus, Docker CLI.

1.4.5 Game Development

Although not as popular as C++ in gaming, Go has game engines like **Ebiten** and **G3N** for **lightweight 2D and 3D game development**.

- **Examples**: Game servers, multiplayer networking.
- **Who Uses It?** Indie developers, small-scale gaming projects.

1.5 Understanding Go's Role in Modern Software Development

With the rise of **cloud computing, microservices, and distributed systems**, developers need programming languages that can handle **scalability, performance, and simplicity**. Go has become a **key player** in this shift.

1.5.1 Go in Cloud Computing

Go powers **cloud platforms** like **Kubernetes, Docker, and Google Cloud** because it is **lightweight and easy to deploy.**

✔ Cloud-native applications run efficiently with **Go's single binary deployment model.**

✔ Microservices written in Go **consume fewer resources** compared to Java or Python.

1.5.2 Go in High-Performance Backend Systems

Go's **efficient concurrency model** makes it ideal for backend services handling **millions of requests.** Many companies use Go for **real-time processing** and **event-driven architectures.**

✔ **Use Cases**: Payment gateways, messaging queues, and analytics processing.

✔ **Who Uses It?** PayPal, Uber, Twitch.

1.5.3 Go in DevOps and Site Reliability Engineering (SRE)

Go has become a top choice for **DevOps tools.** Infrastructure automation, monitoring, and performance tracking tools are often built in Go.

✔ Terraform (Infrastructure-as-Code)

✔ Prometheus (Monitoring)

✔ Docker CLI (Container Management)

1.5.4 The Future of Go

Go continues to evolve, with **Go 2.0** bringing more improvements. It is growing as a **default language** for scalable applications and **will play an even bigger role in the future** of cloud computing, distributed systems, and AI infrastructure.

Go stands out as a **modern, high-performance, and easy-to-learn language** built for today's software challenges. Whether you're working on web applications, cloud services, or networking tools, Go provides **speed, simplicity, and scalability** that few other languages can match.

Chapter 2: Setting Up Your Go Environment

2.1 Installing Go on Windows, Mac, and Linux

Before writing Go programs, you need to **install the Go programming language** on your system. Go provides precompiled binaries for **Windows, macOS, and Linux**, making the installation process straightforward.

This section covers:
✔ Downloading and installing Go on **Windows, macOS, and Linux**
✔ Configuring **environment variables**
✔ Verifying the installation

2.1.1 Downloading Go

To install Go, you must download the latest stable release from the **official Go website**:
☛ https://go.dev/dl/

Go releases are available for **Windows, macOS, and Linux**, with .msi (Windows), .pkg (macOS), and .tar.gz (Linux) packages.

2.1.2 Installing Go on Windows

Step 1: Download the Windows Installer

- Visit https://go.dev/dl/
- Download the **Windows .msi installer** (e.g., go1.x.x.windows-amd64.msi).
- Ensure you download the correct version for **64-bit systems** (most modern computers).

Step 2: Run the Installer

- Open the .msi file and follow the on-screen instructions.

- The installer will:
  - ✔ Install Go in the default directory (C:\Go).
  - ✔ Set up Go's environment variables automatically.

Step 3: Verify Installation

After installation, verify Go is installed correctly:

[1] Open **Command Prompt (cmd)** or **PowerShell**
[2] Run the command:

sh
CopyEdit
```
go version
```

✔ If installed correctly, you will see output like:

sh
CopyEdit
```
go version go1.x.x windows/amd64
```

2.1.3 Installing Go on macOS

Step 1: Download the macOS Installer

- Visit https://go.dev/dl/
- Download the .pkg file (e.g., go1.x.x.darwin-amd64.pkg).

Step 2: Install Go

- Double-click the .pkg file and follow the installation instructions.
- By default, Go is installed in **/usr/local/go**.

Step 3: Verify Installation

☐ Open **Terminal**
☐ Run:

```sh
CopyEdit
go version
```

✔ Expected output:

```sh
CopyEdit
go version go1.x.x darwin/amd64
```

Step 4: Setting Up Go Environment on macOS (Optional)

To ensure Go binaries are accessible system-wide, update your **shell profile**:

For **zsh (default shell on macOS Catalina and later)**:

```sh
CopyEdit
echo 'export PATH=$PATH:/usr/local/go/bin' >> ~/.zshrc
source ~/.zshrc
```

For **bash (older macOS versions)**:

```sh
CopyEdit
echo 'export PATH=$PATH:/usr/local/go/bin' >> ~/.bash_profile
source ~/.bash_profile
```

2.1.4 Installing Go on Linux

Step 1: Download the Go Binary

☐ Open **Terminal** and download the latest Go version (replace x.x with the latest version):

sh
CopyEdit
wget https://go.dev/dl/go1.x.x.linux-amd64.tar.gz

② Extract and install Go:

sh
CopyEdit
sudo tar -C /usr/local -xzf go1.x.x.linux-amd64.tar.gz

This installs Go in **/usr/local/go**.

Step 2: Configure Environment Variables

To use Go system-wide, update the PATH variable:

sh
CopyEdit
echo 'export PATH=$PATH:/usr/local/go/bin' >> ~/.bashrc
source ~/.bashrc

For **zsh users**:

sh
CopyEdit
echo 'export PATH=$PATH:/usr/local/go/bin' >> ~/.zshrc
source ~/.zshrc

Step 3: Verify Installation

Run:

sh
CopyEdit
go version

✔ Expected output:

sh
CopyEdit
go version go1.x.x linux/amd64

2.1.5 Updating Go

To update Go, follow these steps:
1 Remove the existing version:

sh
CopyEdit
sudo rm -rf /usr/local/go

2 Install the latest version using the steps above.

2.2 Understanding the Go Workspace and GOPATH

Once Go is installed, understanding the **Go workspace** and **GOPATH** is essential for organizing and managing Go projects.

2.2.1 What Is the Go Workspace?

The **Go workspace** is the directory where Go projects are stored. In earlier versions of Go (before **Go 1.11**), all projects had to be inside the GOPATH **workspace**. However, with **Go Modules**, this restriction is no longer necessary.

Still, understanding the workspace structure helps in organizing Go projects efficiently.

2.2.2 Understanding GOPATH

What is GOPATH?

The GOPATH environment variable defines the **workspace directory** where Go code, dependencies, and compiled binaries are stored.

Default GOPATH Location

OS	Default GOPATH
Windows	`C:\Users\YourUser\go`
macOS/Linux	`$HOME/go` (`/home/user/go`)

To check the GOPATH, run:

sh
CopyEdit
```
go env GOPATH
```

✔ Expected output (Linux/macOS example):

sh
CopyEdit
```
/home/user/go
```

2.2.3 Go Workspace Structure

The GOPATH workspace typically has three main directories:

bash
CopyEdit
```
$GOPATH/
├── bin/      # Compiled binaries
├── pkg/      # Package objects
├── src/      # Go source code
```

✔ **bin/**: Stores compiled executables from Go projects.
✔ **pkg/**: Holds compiled package files.
✔ **src/**: Contains source code of Go projects.

Each Go project inside src/ follows this structure:

swift
CopyEdit
```
$GOPATH/src/github.com/username/projectname/
├── main.go
├── go.mod
├── README.md
```

2.2.4 Go Modules (Replacing GOPATH)

Since **Go 1.11**, the introduction of **Go Modules** made GOPATH **optional**. Now, Go projects can be created anywhere on the system, and dependencies are managed using **Go Modules** (go.mod and go.sum).

How to Enable Go Modules

1 Navigate to your project directory:

sh
CopyEdit
```
mkdir myproject && cd myproject
```

2 Initialize a new Go module:

sh
CopyEdit
```
go mod init github.com/username/myproject
```

This creates a go.mod file that manages dependencies.

Checking If Go Modules Are Enabled

Run:

sh
CopyEdit
```
go env GO111MODULE
```

✔ If the output is on, Go Modules are active.

2.5 Setting Up a Custom GOPATH (Optional)

If you prefer using a custom workspace, you can manually set the GOPATH:

On Linux/macOS:

Add this to your .bashrc or .zshrc:

sh
CopyEdit
```
export GOPATH=$HOME/mygoprojects
export PATH=$PATH:$GOPATH/bin
```

Then, apply changes:

```sh
CopyEdit
source ~/.bashrc  # or source ~/.zshrc
```

On Windows:

1. Open **Control Panel > System > Advanced System Settings**
2. Click **Environment Variables**
3. Under **System Variables**, add:

- GOPATH = C:\GoWorkspace
- PATH = %GOPATH%\bin

Now that you have Go installed and understand how to structure Go projects using GOPATH and **Go Modules**, you're ready to start coding! Next, we'll write our **first Go program** and explore Go's **basic syntax**.

2.3 Setting Up a Go Development Environment (VS Code, GoLand, Terminal)

A well-configured development environment improves productivity and makes coding in Go easier. Whether you prefer **lightweight editors like VS Code, full-fledged IDEs like GoLand**, or simply working from the **terminal**, Go provides a smooth development experience.

This section covers:
✔ **Setting up Visual Studio Code (VS Code) for Go**

✔ Configuring GoLand (JetBrains IDE)
✔ Using the terminal for Go development

2.3.1 Setting Up VS Code for Go

Visual Studio Code (VS Code) is a popular, lightweight editor with excellent Go support.

Step 1: Install VS Code

- Download VS Code from https://code.visualstudio.com.
- Install it based on your OS (Windows, macOS, Linux).

Step 2: Install the Go Extension

1. Open VS Code and go to **Extensions** (Ctrl+Shift+X or Cmd+Shift+X on Mac).
2. Search for **"Go"** and install the extension developed by **Google**.
3. After installation, restart VS Code.

Step 3: Configure Go in VS Code

To enable auto-formatting, linting, and debugging, modify the Go settings:
1. Open VS Code settings (Ctrl + ,)
2. Search for "go.formatTool" and set it to "gofmt".
3. Search for "go.lintTool" and enable "golint" for best practices.

Step 4: Install Additional Go Tools

To enhance Go development, install essential tools:

sh

CopyEdit

go install golang.org/x/tools/cmd/gopls@latest

go install github.com/uudashr/gopkgs/v2/cmd/gopkgs@latest

go install github.com/ramya-rao-a/go-outline@latest

These tools provide **intellisense, autocompletion, and debugging**.

✔ VS Code is now ready for Go development! ●

2.3.2 Setting Up GoLand for Go

GoLand by **JetBrains** is a powerful IDE specifically designed for Go.

Step 1: Install GoLand

- Download GoLand from https://www.jetbrains.com/go/.
- Follow the installation instructions for your OS.

Step 2: Create a New Go Project

1. Open GoLand
2. Click **New Project** → Select **Go Modules**
3. Choose the project directory and click **Create**

✔ GoLand provides **built-in debugging, linting, and refactoring tools** for professional Go development.

2.3.3 Using the Terminal for Go Development

For minimal setups, Go can be used directly from the **command line**.

Required Tools

- **Text Editor**: Use **Nano, Vim, or Emacs** to write Go code.
- **Terminal Commands**: Use go run, go build, and go fmt (covered later).

✔ Ideal for **lightweight and server-side development**.

2.4 Writing and Running Your First Go Program

Now that your environment is set up, let's write and run your first Go program.

2.4.1 Creating a Go Project

1. Open **VS Code, GoLand, or Terminal**
2. Create a new folder for your project:

sh

CopyEdit

```
mkdir hello-go && cd hello-go
```

3. Initialize a Go module:

sh

CopyEdit

```
go mod init github.com/yourusername/hello-go
```

2.4.2 Writing a Simple Go Program

Inside the **hello-go** folder, create a file named main.go:

go

CopyEdit

```
package main
```

```
import "fmt"

func main() {

    fmt.Println("Hello, Go!")

}
```

✔ **Explanation**:

- package main → Defines the package as an **executable program**.
- import "fmt" → Imports the **fmt package** for printing output.
- func main() → The **entry point** of a Go program.

2.4.3 Running the Go Program

To run the Go program, use:

sh

CopyEdit

```
go run main.go
```

✔ Expected Output:

sh

CopyEdit

```
Hello, Go!
```

2.5 Understanding go run, go build, and go fmt

Go provides several commands to compile, run, and format code. Let's explore their differences.

2.5.1 go run – Execute a Go Program Without Compiling

The go run command **compiles and runs** the Go program **without creating an executable file**.

Usage

sh

CopyEdit

```
go run main.go
```

✔ Best for **testing** small programs.
✔ Not recommended for **production use**.

2.5.2 go build – Compile a Go Program into an Executable

The go build command **compiles** a Go program and generates an executable binary.

Usage

1. Run go build:

sh

CopyEdit

```
go build main.go
```

2. A binary file (main on Linux/macOS or main.exe on Windows) is created.
3. Execute the binary:

sh

CopyEdit

```
./main   # (Linux/macOS)
main.exe # (Windows)
```

✔ Best for **creating production-ready applications**.

2.5.3 go fmt – Format Go Code Properly

Go enforces **consistent code formatting** using go fmt.

Usage

sh

CopyEdit

```
go fmt main.go
```

✔ **Automatically formats** code to follow Go's best practices.
✔ Helps **avoid messy and inconsistent indentation**.

Now, you have:
✔ Installed Go and configured your environment.
✔ Set up **VS Code, GoLand, and Terminal** for development.
✔ Written, executed, and compiled your first Go program.

Chapter 3: Basic Syntax and Fundamentals

3.1 Variables, Constants, and Data Types

Understanding **variables, constants, and data types** is essential in Go, as they determine how data is stored, processed, and manipulated. Go is a **statically typed** language, meaning every variable has a specific type that is determined at **compile time**.

3.1.1 Variables in Go

A **variable** is a storage location that holds a value. In Go, variables are **declared explicitly** or **inferred automatically**. The var keyword is used to declare variables.

Declaring Variables in Go

There are several ways to declare variables in Go:

1. Using the var Keyword (Explicit Type)

```go
CopyEdit
var age int
age = 25
```

- Here, age is declared as an **integer (int)**.
- It is **initialized later** with 25.

2. Using var with Initialization

```go
CopyEdit
var name string = "John Doe"
```

- The type is **explicitly defined** (string).
- The variable is **initialized at the time of declaration**.

3. Using Short Variable Declaration (:=)

Go allows a **shorthand** syntax for declaring and initializing variables.

go
CopyEdit
```
score := 95
```

- The := operator **declares and initializes** score in one step.
- Go **infers** the type based on the value (int in this case).
- This method **can only be used inside functions**.

3.1.2 Constants in Go

A **constant** is a variable whose value cannot change once assigned. Constants are useful for **fixed values** like mathematical constants, configuration values, and API keys.

Declaring Constants

go
CopyEdit
```
const pi float64 = 3.14159
const appName = "Go Application"
```

- Constants are defined using const.
- The type is optional; Go infers it if not specified.

Multiple Constants Declaration

go
CopyEdit
```
const (
    version   = "1.0.0"
    maxUsers  = 100
    debugMode = false
)
```

✔ **Constants cannot be changed after declaration.**

3.1.3 Data Types in Go

Go provides **several data types** categorized into **numeric types, boolean types, string types, and composite types**.

1. Numeric Types

Data Type	Description	Example
`int`	Integer numbers (platform-dependent)	`var a int = 42`
`int8`, `int16`, `int32`, `int64`	Fixed-size integers	`var b int16 = 100`
`uint`, `uint8`, `uint16`, `uint32`, `uint64`	Unsigned integers	`var c uint8 = 255`
`float32`, `float64`	Floating-point numbers	`var d float64 = 3.14`
`complex64`, `complex128`	Complex numbers	`var e complex128 = 2 + 3i`

2. Boolean Type

A boolean variable can only be **true** or **false**.

```go
CopyEdit
var isActive bool = true
```

3. String Type

Strings are sequences of characters enclosed in double quotes ("").

```go
CopyEdit
var greeting string = "Hello, Go!"
```

✔ Strings are **immutable**, meaning they **cannot be changed after creation**.

29

4. Composite Types

Composite types include **arrays, slices, maps, structs, and interfaces**.

Data Type	Description
array	Fixed-size collection of elements of the same type
slice	Dynamic-size array-like structure
map	Key-value pair collection
struct	User-defined data structure
interface	Defines a set of method signatures

3.2 Operators and Expressions in Go

Operators are used to perform operations on **variables and values**. Go supports **arithmetic, comparison, logical, bitwise, and assignment operators**.

3.2.1 Arithmetic Operators

Arithmetic operators perform **basic mathematical operations**.

Operator	Description	Example
+	Addition	x + y
-	Subtraction	x - y
*	Multiplication	x * y
/	Division	x / y
%	Modulus (Remainder)	x % y

Example Usage

go
CopyEdit
```
x := 10
y := 3
```

```
sum := x + y      // 13
difference := x - y // 7
product := x * y   // 30
quotient := x / y  // 3 (integer division)
remainder := x % y // 1
```

✔ **Integer division in Go truncates the decimal part**.

3.2.2 Comparison Operators

Comparison operators compare **two values** and return a boolean (true or false).

Operator	Description	Example
==	Equal to	x == y
!=	Not equal to	x != y
>	Greater than	x > y
<	Less than	x < y
>=	Greater than or equal to	x >= y
<=	Less than or equal to	x <= y

Example Usage

go
CopyEdit
```
a := 5
b := 10

fmt.Println(a == b) // false
fmt.Println(a != b) // true
fmt.Println(a < b)  // true
fmt.Println(a > b)  // false
```

3.2.3 Logical Operators

Logical operators are used in **boolean expressions**.

Operator	Description	Example
&&	Logical AND	(x > 5) && (y < 10)
`		
!	Logical NOT	!(x > y)

Example Usage

go
CopyEdit
isAdult := true
hasID := false

fmt.Println(isAdult && hasID) // false
fmt.Println(isAdult || hasID) // true
fmt.Println(!isAdult)   // false

✔ && requires **both** conditions to be true.
✔ || requires **at least one** condition to be true.

3.2.4 Bitwise Operators

Bitwise operators work at the **binary level**.

Operator	Description	Example
&	AND	x & y
`	`	OR
^	XOR	x ^ y
<<	Left shift	x << 2
>>	Right shift	x >> 2

32

Example Usage

```go
x := 5  // 0101 in binary
y := 3  // 0011 in binary

fmt.Println(x & y)  // 0001 → 1
fmt.Println(x | y)  // 0111 → 7
fmt.Println(x ^ y)  // 0110 → 6
```

3.2.5 Assignment Operators

Assignment operators **assign values** to variables.

Operator	Description	Example
=	Assign	x = 10
+=	Add and assign	x += 5 (x = x + 5)
-=	Subtract and assign	x -= 5 (x = x - 5)
*=	Multiply and assign	x *= 5 (x = x * 5)
/=	Divide and assign	x /= 5 (x = x / 5)
%=	Modulus and assign	x %= 5 (x = x % 5)

Example Usage

```go
x := 10
x += 5  // x = 15
x -= 2  // x = 13
x *= 2  // x = 26
x /= 2  // x = 13
```

33

3.3 Type Conversion and Type Inference

In Go, variables have **fixed data types** once declared, meaning you cannot assign values of different types to a variable without **explicit conversion**. This is because Go is a **statically typed** language.

3.3.1 Type Conversion in Go

Type conversion is the process of **manually converting** a value from one data type to another. In Go, this is done using **explicit type conversion**.

Syntax for Type Conversion

go

CopyEdit

```
convertedValue := DataType(originalValue)
```

Example: Converting int to float64

go

CopyEdit

```
var x int = 42
var y float64 = float64(x)  // Convert int to float64


fmt.Println(y)  // Output: 42.0
```

34

✔ Go does not allow **implicit type conversion**, so you must explicitly cast between types.

3.3.2 Common Type Conversions

Conversion	Example
int → float64	float64(x)
float64 → int	int(y) (truncates decimal)
string → int	strconv.Atoi(str)
int → string	strconv.Itoa(num)

Example: Converting string to int

go

CopyEdit

```
import "strconv"


str := "100"

num, err := strconv.Atoi(str)  // Convert string to int

if err == nil {

    fmt.Println(num)  // Output: 100

}
```

Example: Converting int to string

go

CopyEdit

```
import "strconv"
```

35

```
num := 50

str := strconv.Itoa(num)  // Convert int to string


fmt.Println(str)  // Output: "50"
```

3.3.3 Type Inference in Go

Go **infers types** automatically when using the := operator.

go

CopyEdit

```
name := "Alice"   // Inferred as string

age := 30        // Inferred as int

height := 5.9    // Inferred as float64
```

✔ **Benefits of Type Inference**:

- Reduces redundancy.
- Makes code cleaner and more readable.
- Prevents unnecessary type declarations.

3.4 Reading Input and Printing Output

Programs often **interact with users** by reading input and printing output. Go provides multiple ways to handle **input and output (I/O)** operations.

36

3.4.1 Printing Output in Go

Go uses the fmt package for printing to the console.

Basic Print Statements

go

CopyEdit

```
fmt.Print("Hello, ")

fmt.Println("World!")
```

✔ Output:

CopyEdit

```
Hello, World!
```

- fmt.Print() prints without adding a newline.
- fmt.Println() **automatically adds a newline** at the end.

Printing Formatted Output

Go supports formatted printing using fmt.Printf().

go

CopyEdit

```
name := "Alice"

age := 25

fmt.Printf("Name: %s, Age: %d\n", name, age)
```

✔ Output:

yaml

CopyEdit

Name: Alice, Age: 25

- %s → String placeholder.
- %d → Integer placeholder.
- \n → Newline character.

Common Format Specifiers

Specifier	Description	Example
%d	Integer	fmt.Printf("%d", 10)
%f	Floating-point number	fmt.Printf("%f", 3.14)
%s	String	fmt.Printf("%s", "hello")
%t	Boolean	fmt.Printf("%t", true)
%v	Any type	fmt.Printf("%v", value)

3.4.2 Reading Input from the User

Go provides several ways to read input from the user.

Reading Input with fmt.Scan

The fmt.Scan() function reads input **until whitespace** is encountered.

go

CopyEdit

var name string

fmt.Print("Enter your name: ")

38

```
fmt.Scan(&name) // Read input

fmt.Println("Hello,", name)
```

✔ **Example Input:**

yaml

CopyEdit

```
Enter your name: Alice
Hello, Alice
```

✔ **Note:** Scan() stops reading at the first space.

Reading Full Line Input with fmt.Scanln

To read a **full line** of input:

go

CopyEdit

```
var fullName string
fmt.Print("Enter your full name: ")
fmt.Scanln(&fullName)

fmt.Println("Your name is:", fullName)
```

✔ This method still has **limitations** because it stops at the first whitespace.

Reading Multiple Values with fmt.Scanf

Use fmt.Scanf() for formatted input.

go

CopyEdit

```go
var name string

var age int

fmt.Print("Enter name and age: ")

fmt.Scanf("%s %d", &name, &age)


fmt.Printf("Name: %s, Age: %d\n", name, age)
```

✔ **Example Input:**

yaml

CopyEdit

```yaml
Enter name and age: Alice 25
```

✔ **Output:**

yaml

CopyEdit

```yaml
Name: Alice, Age: 25
```

3.5 Understanding the fmt Package

The fmt package is the **standard Go library** for formatting and printing output. It provides functions for: ✔ Printing text to the console.
✔ Reading input from the user.
✔ Formatting strings with placeholders.

3.5.1 Common fmt Functions

Function	Description	Example
fmt.Print()	Print without newline	fmt.Print("Hello")
fmt.Println()	Print with newline	fmt.Println("Hello")
fmt.Printf()	Print formatted text	fmt.Printf("Age: %d", 30)
fmt.Scan()	Read input (single word)	fmt.Scan(&name)
fmt.Scanln()	Read input (full line)	fmt.Scanln(&name)
fmt.Scanf()	Read formatted input	fmt.Scanf("%s %d", &name, &age)

3.5.2 Using fmt.Sprintf for String Formatting

fmt.Sprintf() returns a formatted string **without printing it**.

go

CopyEdit

name := "Alice"

age := 25

message := fmt.Sprintf("Name: %s, Age: %d", name, age)

fmt.Println(message)

✔ Output:

yaml

CopyEdit

Name: Alice, Age: 25

✔ Useful for **storing formatted strings in variables**.

3.5.3 Using fmt.Errorf for Error Handling

fmt.Errorf() allows creating **custom error messages**.

go

CopyEdit

```
import "fmt"


err := fmt.Errorf("file not found: %s", "document.txt")

fmt.Println(err)
```

✔ Output:

javascript

CopyEdit

file not found: document.txt

✔ Helpful for logging meaningful error messages.

42

Now that you understand **type conversion, input/output handling, and the** fmt **package**, you can build **interactive and formatted** Go programs.

Chapter 4: Control Flow and Loops

Control flow statements allow programs to **make decisions** and **execute repetitive tasks** efficiently. Go provides **conditional statements** like if-else and switch for decision-making and **looping constructs** like for and range for iteration.

4.1 Conditional Statements (if-else, switch)

Conditional statements allow the execution of different code blocks based on **specific conditions**.

4.1.1 The if Statement

The if statement evaluates a **Boolean condition** and executes a block of code if the condition is true.

Syntax
go
CopyEdit
```
if condition {
    // Code to execute if the condition is true
}
```

Example: Checking if a Number is Positive
go
CopyEdit
```
num := 10

if num > 0 {
    fmt.Println("The number is positive")
}
```

✔ **If num is greater than 0**, the message is printed.

4.1.2 The if-else Statement

The if-else statement **executes one block if the condition is true** and another block **if it is false**.

Syntax
go
CopyEdit
```
if condition {
    // Code executes if condition is true
} else {
    // Code executes if condition is false
}
```

Example: Checking if a Number is Positive or Negative
go
CopyEdit
```
num := -5

if num > 0 {
    fmt.Println("Positive number")
} else {
    fmt.Println("Negative number")
}
```

✔ **Since num is negative, the second block runs.**

4.1.3 The if-else if-else Statement

When multiple conditions need to be checked, use else if.

Syntax

```go
if condition1 {
    // Executes if condition1 is true
} else if condition2 {
    // Executes if condition2 is true
} else {
    // Executes if none of the conditions are true
}
```

Example: Grading System

```go
score := 85

if score >= 90 {
    fmt.Println("Grade: A")
} else if score >= 80 {
    fmt.Println("Grade: B")
} else if score >= 70 {
    fmt.Println("Grade: C")
} else {
    fmt.Println("Grade: F")
}
```

✔ **This evaluates multiple conditions to determine the grade.**

4.1.4 The switch Statement

A switch statement provides a **cleaner** alternative to multiple if-else conditions.

Syntax

```go
switch value {
case case1:
```

```
    // Executes if value matches case1
case case2:
    // Executes if value matches case2
default:
    // Executes if no case matches
}
```

Example: Checking a Day of the Week

go
CopyEdit
```
day := "Tuesday"

switch day {
case "Monday":
    fmt.Println("Start of the work week!")
case "Friday":
    fmt.Println("Almost weekend!")
case "Saturday", "Sunday":
    fmt.Println("It's the weekend!")
default:
    fmt.Println("It's a regular weekday.")
}
```

✔ Switch checks the day variable and executes the matching case.
✔ Multiple cases (Saturday, Sunday) can share the same execution block.

4.1.5 The switch with fallthrough

By default, a switch statement in Go **does not fall through** to the next case. However, fallthrough can be used to continue execution to the next case.

Example

go
CopyEdit
```
num := 2
```

```go
switch num {
case 1:
    fmt.Println("One")
case 2:
    fmt.Println("Two")
    fallthrough
case 3:
    fmt.Println("Three")  // This executes because of fallthrough
default:
    fmt.Println("Other number")
}
```

✔ **Without fallthrough, the second case (Two) would execute, and execution would stop.**
✔ **With fallthrough, it continues executing the next case (Three).**

4.1.6 The switch Without an Expression

A switch can also be used like multiple if-else statements.

Example

go
CopyEdit
```go
num := 15

switch {
case num < 0:
    fmt.Println("Negative number")
case num > 0 && num < 10:
    fmt.Println("Single-digit number")
default:
    fmt.Println("Number has multiple digits")
}
```

✔ The switch statement evaluates each case as a Boolean condition.

4.2 Loops in Go (for, range)

Loops **execute a block of code multiple times**. Unlike other languages, Go only has **one loop type: for.**

4.2.1 The for Loop

A for loop runs a block of code **as long as a condition is true**.

Syntax

go
CopyEdit
```
for initialization; condition; post {
    // Code to execute
}
```

Example: Printing Numbers from 1 to 5

go
CopyEdit
```
for i := 1; i <= 5; i++ {
    fmt.Println(i)
}
```

✔ i := 1 → Initializes the loop variable.
✔ i <= 5 → Condition to continue looping.
✔ i++ → Increments i in each iteration.

4.2.2 The for Loop Without Initialization and Post Statements

Go allows for loops with **only a condition**, making it behave like a while loop.

49

Example: Countdown from 5

go
CopyEdit

```
i := 5

for i > 0 {
    fmt.Println(i)
    i--
}
```

✔ This loop runs until i reaches 0.
✔ Commonly used for infinite loops when the termination condition is inside the loop.

4.2.3 The Infinite for Loop

A loop **without a condition** runs **forever**.

Example: Infinite Loop

go
CopyEdit

```
for {
    fmt.Println("This will run forever")
}
```

✔ Used for servers, background tasks, or event listeners.
✔ Must include a break statement to stop execution.

4.2.4 Breaking Out of a Loop (break)

Use break to **exit a loop early**.

Example: Stopping When i Reaches 3
go
CopyEdit
```
for i := 1; i <= 5; i++ {
   if i == 3 {
      break  // Exit the loop
   }
   fmt.Println(i)
}
```

✔ **Loop terminates when i equals 3.**

4.2.5 Skipping an Iteration (continue)

The continue statement **skips the current iteration** and moves to the next one.

Example: Skipping Even Numbers
go
CopyEdit
```
for i := 1; i <= 5; i++ {
   if i%2 == 0 {
      continue  // Skip even numbers
   }
   fmt.Println(i)
}
```

✔ **Even numbers are skipped.**
✔ **Loop continues execution for other values.**

4.2.6 The range Loop (Iterating Over Collections)

The range keyword simplifies iteration over collections like **arrays, slices, maps, and strings**.

Example: Iterating Over an Array

go
CopyEdit
```go
numbers := []int{10, 20, 30, 40, 50}

for index, value := range numbers {
    fmt.Printf("Index: %d, Value: %d\n", index, value)
}
```

✔ range **returns both index and value.**
✔ Use _ **to ignore the index or value.**

4.2.7 Iterating Over a Map

go
CopyEdit
```go
cities := map[string]string{
    "NY": "New York",
    "SF": "San Francisco",
}

for key, value := range cities {
    fmt.Printf("%s -> %s\n", key, value)
}
```

✔ **Useful for processing key-value pairs.**

You've learned how to **control the flow of execution** in Go using: ✔ if-else for decision-making.

✔ switch for multiple conditions.

✔ for loops for iteration.

4.3 Nested Loops and Loop Control Statements (break, continue)

4.3.1 Nested Loops in Go

A **nested loop** is a loop inside another loop. This is useful when working with **multi-dimensional arrays, generating patterns, or processing hierarchical data**.

Example: Printing a Multiplication Table

go

CopyEdit

```
for i := 1; i <= 3; i++ {

  for j := 1; j <= 3; j++ {

    fmt.Printf("%d x %d = %d\n", i, j, i*j)

  }

}
```

✔ **The outer loop (i) runs three times.**
✔ **The inner loop (j) runs for each i, producing a multiplication table.**

4.3.2 Using break in Loops

The break statement **immediately exits the loop** when a condition is met.

Example: Stopping a Loop When a Condition is Met

go

CopyEdit

```
for i := 1; i <= 10; i++ {
   if i == 5 {
      break  // Exit loop when i reaches 5
   }
   fmt.Println(i)
}
```

✔ **Output:**

CopyEdit

```
1
2
3
4
```

✔ The loop **stops when** i == 5.

4.3.3 Using continue to Skip an Iteration

The continue statement **skips the current iteration** and moves to the next one.

Example: Skipping Even Numbers

go

CopyEdit

```go
for i := 1; i <= 5; i++ {
    if i%2 == 0 {
        continue  // Skip even numbers
    }
    fmt.Println(i)
}
```

✔ **Output:**

CopyEdit

```
1
3
5
```

✔ **Even numbers (2, 4) are skipped.**

4.3.4 Using break and continue in Nested Loops

In nested loops, break exits the **innermost loop**, while continue skips **only the current iteration of the innermost loop**.

Example: Breaking Out of Nested Loops

go

CopyEdit

```go
for i := 1; i <= 3; i++ {
    for j := 1; j <= 3; j++ {
        if j == 2 {
            break  // Breaks only the inner loop
        }
        fmt.Printf("i = %d, j = %d\n", i, j)
    }
}
```

✔ **Output:**

ini

CopyEdit

```ini
i = 1, j = 1
i = 2, j = 1
i = 3, j = 1
```

✔ The **inner loop stops when j == 2**, but the **outer loop continues**.

Example: Skipping an Iteration in a Nested Loop

go

CopyEdit

```
for i := 1; i <= 3; i++ {
    for j := 1; j <= 3; j++ {
        if j == 2 {
            continue  // Skip j == 2
        }
        fmt.Printf("i = %d, j = %d\n", i, j)
    }
}
```

✔ **Output:**

ini

CopyEdit

```
i = 1, j = 1
i = 1, j = 3
i = 2, j = 1
i = 2, j = 3
i = 3, j = 1
i = 3, j = 3
```

✔ When j == 2, the iteration is skipped, and j == 3 runs next.

4.4 Error Handling with panic and recover

Go provides robust **error handling mechanisms**, with panic and recover allowing programs to **handle unexpected errors** gracefully.

4.4.1 Understanding panic in Go

A **panic** occurs when a Go program encounters a **critical error** that prevents further execution.

Common scenarios where panic is used: ✔ Accessing an **out-of-bounds** array index.
✔ Dereferencing a **nil pointer**.
✔ **Manually triggering a panic** in case of an unexpected failure.

Example: Triggering a Panic

go

CopyEdit

```
func main() {
    fmt.Println("Before panic")
    panic("Something went wrong!")  // Trigger panic
    fmt.Println("After panic")      // This line will not execute
}
```

✔ Output:

go

CopyEdit

Before panic

panic: Something went wrong!

✔ Program execution stops immediately after panic.

4.4.2 Handling Panic with recover

The recover() function **recovers from a panic,** preventing the program from crashing.

Example: Using recover to Handle Panic Gracefully

go

CopyEdit

```
func main() {
    defer handlePanic() // Defer execution of error handler
    fmt.Println("Before panic")
    panic("Unexpected error!") // Triggers panic
    fmt.Println("After panic") // This will not execute
}


func handlePanic() {
    if r := recover(); r != nil {
```

```
        fmt.Println("Recovered from panic:", r)

    }

}
```

✔ Output:

go

CopyEdit

Before panic

Recovered from panic: Unexpected error!

✔ recover() **catches the panic and allows the program to continue.**

4.4.3 Using defer, panic, and recover Together

The defer statement ensures a function is executed **before a function exits**, making it useful for cleanup tasks.

Example: Recovering from a Panic in a Deferred Function

go

CopyEdit

```
func divide(a, b int) {

    defer func() {

        if r := recover(); r != nil {

            fmt.Println("Recovered from panic:", r)
```

```go
    }

    }()

    if b == 0 {

        panic("Cannot divide by zero!") // Trigger panic

    }

    fmt.Println("Result:", a/b)

}

func main() {

    divide(10, 0) // Causes panic

    fmt.Println("Program continues after panic recovery")

}
```

✔ **Output:**

pgsql

CopyEdit

Recovered from panic: Cannot divide by zero!

Program continues after panic recovery

✔ The **program doesn't crash** because recover() **catches the panic.**

61

4.4.4 When to Use panic and recover

◼ **When to use panic:**

- **Unexpected critical errors** (e.g., database connection failures, disk corruption).
- **Developing libraries** where unexpected behavior should be reported immediately.

◼ **When to use recover:**

- **Graceful recovery** from panics (e.g., handling failed API requests).
- **Logging errors** while keeping the system running.

✘ **Avoid using panic for:**

- Regular **error handling** (use errors.New() or fmt.Errorf() instead).
- **User input validation** (return an error instead of panicking).

You now understand: ✔ **Nested loops** for complex iterations.
✔ **Loop control (break, continue)** to manage execution.
✔ **Panic handling** with panic and recover.

Chapter 5: Functions and Error Handling

Functions are the building blocks of Go programs, allowing code to be organized, reusable, and maintainable. Well-structured functions make programs easier to read, debug, and scale. This chapter covers how to define and use functions, pass parameters, return values, and write idiomatic Go functions.

5.1 Writing and Using Functions

A **function** in Go is a block of code that performs a specific task. Functions **reduce redundancy**, **organize logic**, and **improve code reusability**.

5.1.1 Defining a Function in Go

A function is defined using the func keyword, followed by a **name**, optional **parameters**, and an optional **return value**.

Basic Function Syntax

go
CopyEdit
```
func functionName() {
    // Function body (logic)
}
```

Example: A Simple Function

go
CopyEdit
```
func greet() {
    fmt.Println("Hello, welcome to Go!")
}
```

✔ **This function prints a message but doesn't return any value.**

Calling a Function

To execute a function, call it by name:

```go
CopyEdit
func main() {
   greet()  // Function call
}
```

✔ **Output:**

```css
CopyEdit
Hello, welcome to Go!
```

5.1.2 Why Use Functions?

✔ **Code Reusability** – Avoid duplicate code by calling the same function multiple times.
✔ **Readability** – Organize logic into modular units.
✔ **Easier Debugging** – Isolate issues within a specific function.
✔ **Scalability** – Manage complex programs efficiently.

5.1.3 Function with a Parameter

Functions can accept **parameters**, allowing data to be passed when the function is called.

Example: Function with One Parameter

```go
CopyEdit
func greetUser(name string) {
   fmt.Println("Hello,", name)
}
```

64

```go
func main() {
    greetUser("Alice")  // Output: Hello, Alice
    greetUser("Bob")    // Output: Hello, Bob
}
```

✔ Here, name is a parameter of type string.
✔ Each function call passes a different argument.

5.1.4 Function with Multiple Parameters

A function can take multiple parameters, separated by commas.

Example: Function with Two Parameters

go
CopyEdit

```go
func add(a int, b int) {
    fmt.Println("Sum:", a+b)
}

func main() {
    add(5, 10) // Output: Sum: 15
}
```

✔ Both parameters a and b are integers.
✔ Values are passed when calling the function.

🔖 Go allows defining multiple parameters of the same type compactly:

go
CopyEdit

```go
func multiply(x, y int) int {
    return x * y
}
```

65

✔ Here, x and y **share the** int **type.**

5.2 Function Parameters and Return Values

A function can **return a value** after performing a computation.

5.2.1 Function with a Return Value

A function that **returns a value** must specify the return type.

Example: Function That Returns a Value
go
CopyEdit
```
func square(num int) int {
    return num * num
}

func main() {
    result := square(4)
    fmt.Println("Square of 4:", result)
}
```

✔ **The function** square **takes an integer (**num**) and returns an integer (**int**).**
✔ **The** return **keyword sends the computed value back to the caller.**

5.2.2 Multiple Return Values

Go allows **returning multiple values** from a function.

Example: Function That Returns Two Values
go
CopyEdit
```
func divide(dividend, divisor int) (int, int) {
```

```go
    quotient := dividend / divisor
    remainder := dividend % divisor
    return quotient, remainder
}

func main() {
    q, r := divide(10, 3)
    fmt.Println("Quotient:", q, "Remainder:", r)
}
```

✔ **Returns both quotient and remainder.**
✔ **Multiple values are assigned using** q, r := divide(10, 3).

5.2.3 Named Return Values

Go allows **naming return variables,** making the code more readable.

Example: Named Return Values
go
CopyEdit
```go
func calculateRectangle(length, width int) (area, perimeter int) {
    area = length * width
    perimeter = 2 * (length + width)
    return
}

func main() {
    a, p := calculateRectangle(5, 10)
    fmt.Println("Area:", a, "Perimeter:", p)
}
```

✔ **No need to explicitly use** return area, perimeter **since they are pre-declared.**
✔ **Named return values improve clarity.**

5.2.4 Function with Variadic Parameters

A **variadic function** can accept **multiple arguments** of the same type.

Example: Function That Accepts Multiple Arguments

go
CopyEdit

```
func sum(numbers ...int) int {
    total := 0
    for _, num := range numbers {
        total += num
    }
    return total
}

func main() {
    fmt.Println("Sum:", sum(1, 2, 3, 4, 5))  // Output: Sum: 15
}
```

✔ The **...int** syntax allows passing multiple integers.
✔ The function processes all arguments inside a for loop.

5.2.5 Function as a Parameter

Go allows passing functions as parameters, enabling **higher-order functions**.

Example: Function Taking Another Function as Parameter

go
CopyEdit

```
func applyOperation(a, b int, operation func(int, int) int) int {
    return operation(a, b)
}

func multiply(x, y int) int {
    return x * y
}
```

```
func main() {
    result := applyOperation(5, 3, multiply)
    fmt.Println("Multiplication Result:", result)  // Output: 15
}
```

✔ **applyOperation receives a function as a parameter.**
✔ **We pass multiply as an argument to applyOperation().**

5.2.6 Anonymous Functions

Go supports **anonymous functions**, which are functions **without a name**.

Example: Anonymous Function
go
CopyEdit
```
func main() {
    sum := func(a, b int) int {
        return a + b
    }

    fmt.Println("Sum:", sum(5, 7))
}
```

✔ **Useful for short-lived functions.**

Example: Immediately Invoked Function
go
CopyEdit
```
func main() {
    result := func(x, y int) int {
        return x * y
    }(4, 5)  // Function is called immediately

    fmt.Println("Result:", result)
}
```

✔ No need to separately define and call the function.

5.2.7 Recursive Functions

A function that calls itself is called a **recursive function**.

Example: Factorial Using Recursion

go
CopyEdit
```go
func factorial(n int) int {
    if n == 0 {
        return 1
    }
    return n * factorial(n-1)
}

func main() {
    fmt.Println("Factorial of 5:", factorial(5))
}
```

✔ Each function call decreases n until it reaches 0.
✔ Base case (if n == 0) prevents infinite recursion.

You have learned:
✔ How to define and call functions.
✔ Passing parameters and returning values.
✔ Variadic, anonymous, and higher-order functions.
✔ Using recursion effectively

5.3 Multiple Return Values in Go

Go allows functions to return multiple values, which is useful for scenarios where a function needs to return multiple results (e.g., an operation result and an error message).

5.3.1 Basic Syntax for Multiple Return Values

A function can return multiple values by specifying multiple return types in the function signature.

Example: Returning Two Values

go

CopyEdit

```go
func divide(a, b int) (int, int) {
    quotient := a / b
    remainder := a % b
    return quotient, remainder
}


func main() {
    q, r := divide(10, 3)
    fmt.Println("Quotient:", q, "Remainder:", r)
}
```

✔ Function returns both the quotient and remainder.
✔ Caller captures both values using q, r := divide(10, 3).

5.3.2 Ignoring Unused Return Values

If a function returns values that are not needed, use _ (underscore) to ignore them.

Example: Ignoring the Remainder

go

CopyEdit

```
q, _ := divide(10, 3)

fmt.Println("Quotient:", q)
```

✔ The remainder is ignored using _.

5.3.3 Returning a Value and an Error

Many Go functions return both a value and an error to indicate success or failure.

Example: Safe Division Handling Zero-Division

go

CopyEdit

```
func safeDivide(a, b int) (int, error) {

    if b == 0 {

        return 0, fmt.Errorf("cannot divide by zero")

    }
```

```go
    return a / b, nil

}


func main() {

    result, err := safeDivide(10, 0)

    if err != nil {

        fmt.Println("Error:", err)

    } else {

        fmt.Println("Result:", result)

    }

}
```

✔ If b == 0, the function returns an error instead of crashing.
✔ nil means there is no error when the operation succeeds.

5.4 Anonymous Functions and Closures

Go supports anonymous functions, which are functions without a name. These are useful for quick, short-lived operations or when passing functions as arguments.

5.4.1 Declaring an Anonymous Function

Anonymous functions are assigned to a variable and can be called like normal functions.

Example: Storing a Function in a Variable

go

CopyEdit

```
func main() {

   sum := func(a, b int) int {

      return a + b

   }


   fmt.Println("Sum:", sum(4, 6))

}
```

✔ **The function has no name and is stored in** sum.
✔ **Useful for defining functions on-the-fly.**

5.4.2 Immediately Invoked Function Expressions (IIFE)

Anonymous functions can be called immediately after definition.

Example: Immediate Execution

go

CopyEdit

```
func main() {

   result := func(a, b int) int {

      return a * b

   }(3, 4)  // Function is executed immediately
```

```go
fmt.Println("Multiplication Result:", result)

}
```

✔ No need to store the function in a variable.
✔ Useful for quick, one-time operations.

5.4.3 Closures in Go

A closure is an anonymous function that remembers the variables from its surrounding scope.

Example: Using a Closure to Capture State

go

CopyEdit

```go
func counter() func() int {

    count := 0

    return func() int {

        count++

        return count

    }

}


func main() {

    increment := counter()  // Each call to counter() gets a new function

    fmt.Println(increment()) // Output: 1
```

```
fmt.Println(increment())  // Output: 2
```

}

✔ The returned function retains access to count, even after counter() finishes execution.
✔ Useful for stateful computations (e.g., tracking function calls, caching values).

5.5 Error Handling Best Practices

Go encourages explicit error handling instead of exceptions. Go's error type allows functions to return errors alongside results, making error detection explicit and predictable.

5.5.1 The error Type in Go

Errors in Go are represented by the error type.

Example: Returning an Error

go

CopyEdit

```go
func divide(a, b int) (int, error) {

    if b == 0 {

        return 0, fmt.Errorf("cannot divide by zero")

    }

    return a / b, nil

}
```

✔ Returning error makes it clear that an issue may occur.
✔ Using fmt.Errorf() provides a formatted error message.

5.5.2 Checking and Handling Errors

Go uses explicit error checking instead of exceptions.

Example: Checking for an Error

go

CopyEdit

```go
func main() {
    result, err := divide(10, 0)
    if err != nil {
        fmt.Println("Error:", err)
    } else {
        fmt.Println("Result:", result)
    }
}
```

✔ If err is not nil, an error occurred, and the program can handle it.
✔ This approach prevents unexpected crashes.

5.5.3 Defining Custom Errors

Go allows defining custom error types using errors.New().

Example: Custom Error Creation

go

CopyEdit

```go
import "errors"

var ErrZeroDivision = errors.New("cannot divide by zero")

func divide(a, b int) (int, error) {
    if b == 0 {
        return 0, ErrZeroDivision
    }
    return a / b, nil
}

func main() {
    _, err := divide(10, 0)
    if err == ErrZeroDivision {
        fmt.Println("Custom Error:", err)
    }
}
```

✔ Useful for defining reusable error messages.

5.5.4 Error Wrapping with fmt.Errorf

Go allows wrapping errors to add more context.

Example: Wrapping an Error Message

go

CopyEdit

```go
func openFile(filename string) error {

    return fmt.Errorf("failed to open file %s: %w", filename, errors.New("file not found"))

}


func main() {

    err := openFile("data.txt")

    fmt.Println(err)

}
```

✔ %w allows wrapping an underlying error inside a new one.
✔ Useful for debugging by preserving the original error message.

5.5.5 Using panic and recover for Critical Errors

panic should be avoided for normal errors but used for unexpected critical failures.

Example: Recovering from a Panic

go

CopyEdit

```go
func handlePanic() {
    if r := recover(); r != nil {
        fmt.Println("Recovered from panic:", r)
    }
}


func main() {
    defer handlePanic()
    panic("Unexpected failure!")  // Simulating a panic
}
```

✔ recover() **prevents the program from crashing.**
✔ **Use** panic **only for unrecoverable errors, like corrupt memory states.**

Now you understand:
✔ **How to return multiple values in Go functions.**
✔ **Using anonymous functions and closures.**
✔ **Best practices for handling errors gracefully**

Chapter 6: Working with Collections in Go

Go provides several ways to store and manipulate collections of data efficiently. The three main collection types are **arrays, slices, and maps**. Arrays and slices store **sequential data**, while maps provide **key-value pairs** for fast lookups.

6.1 Arrays and Slices (Differences and Use Cases)

Both **arrays** and **slices** are used to store ordered collections of elements, but they have significant differences in terms of **flexibility, size, and use cases**.

6.1.1 Understanding Arrays in Go

An **array** in Go is a **fixed-size, contiguous block of memory** that holds elements of the **same type**. Arrays have a **fixed length** that cannot be changed after declaration.

Syntax for Declaring an Array

go
CopyEdit
```
var arr [5]int  // Declares an integer array with a fixed size of 5
```

✔ **The size (5) is mandatory when declaring an array.**

Example: Initializing an Array

go
CopyEdit
```
var numbers [3]int = [3]int{10, 20, 30}
```

✔ **An array of size 3, initialized with values {10, 20, 30}.**

Shorthand Array Declaration

go
CopyEdit
```
numbers := [4]int{5, 10, 15, 20}
```

✔ The := shorthand makes declaration concise.

Letting Go Infer the Array Size

go
CopyEdit
```
scores := [...]int{90, 80, 85}
fmt.Println(scores)  // Output: [90 80 85]
```

✔ The [...] syntax allows Go to determine the size automatically.

6.1.2 Accessing and Modifying Array Elements

Array elements are accessed **by index**, starting from 0.

Example: Accessing Elements

go
CopyEdit
```
arr := [3]string{"Apple", "Banana", "Cherry"}
fmt.Println(arr[0])  // Output: Apple
fmt.Println(arr[1])  // Output: Banana
```

✔ Indexing starts at 0 (zero-based indexing).

Example: Modifying Elements

go
CopyEdit
```
arr[1] = "Blueberry"
fmt.Println(arr)  // Output: [Apple Blueberry Cherry]
```

✔ **Updates the second element (index 1) to "Blueberry".**

6.1.3 Iterating Over an Array

Arrays can be looped using a for loop.

Using a for Loop

go
CopyEdit

```
numbers := [3]int{2, 4, 6}

for i := 0; i < len(numbers); i++ {
    fmt.Println(numbers[i])
}
```

✔ **Iterates through each index using len(numbers).**

Using range to Iterate

go
CopyEdit

```
for index, value := range numbers {
    fmt.Printf("Index: %d, Value: %d\n", index, value)
}
```

✔ **range returns both the index and value.**
✔ **Use _ to ignore the index:**

go
CopyEdit

```
for _, value := range numbers {
    fmt.Println(value)
}
```

6.1.4 Limitations of Arrays

🪓 **Arrays in Go have some limitations:** ✔ **Fixed Size** – The length **cannot** be changed after declaration.
✔ **Inefficient for Dynamic Data** – Not suitable for dynamically growing lists.

To overcome these limitations, Go provides **slices**.

6.1.5 Understanding Slices in Go

A **slice** is a **dynamic, resizable** collection that provides a more flexible alternative to arrays. Unlike arrays, slices **do not have a fixed size**.

Declaring a Slice
go
CopyEdit
var slice []int // Declares an empty slice

✔ **No size is specified, making it flexible.**

Initializing a Slice with Values
go
CopyEdit
fruits := []string{"Apple", "Banana", "Cherry"}
fmt.Println(fruits) // Output: [Apple Banana Cherry]

✔ **Unlike arrays, slices do not require a fixed length.**

6.1.6 Creating a Slice from an Array

Slices can be **created from arrays** using **slice expressions**.

Example: Slicing an Array
go
CopyEdit
arr := [5]int{1, 2, 3, 4, 5}

84

```
slice := arr[1:4]  // Slice from index 1 to 3 (excludes index 4)
fmt.Println(slice)  // Output: [2 3 4]
```

✔ **arr[start:end]** includes **start** but excludes **end**.

Example: Omitting Start or End Index

go
CopyEdit
```
fmt.Println(arr[:3])  // First 3 elements: [1 2 3]
fmt.Println(arr[2:])  // Elements from index 2 onwards: [3 4 5]
```

6.1.7 Expanding Slices with append()

Slices **can grow dynamically** using append().

Example: Adding Elements to a Slice

go
CopyEdit
```
numbers := []int{10, 20, 30}
numbers = append(numbers, 40, 50)
fmt.Println(numbers)  // Output: [10 20 30 40 50]
```

✔ **append()** returns a new slice with added elements.

6.1.8 Differences Between Arrays and Slices

Feature	Arrays	Slices
Size	Fixed-length	Dynamic size
Flexibility	Cannot grow/shrink	Can expand using `append()`
Performance	More memory-efficient for fixed-size data	More flexible for dynamic data

✔ **Use arrays when working with a fixed-size dataset.**
✔ **Use slices for dynamic collections.**

```
```

6.2 Working with Maps (Key-Value Pairs)

A **map** is a collection of **key-value pairs**, similar to dictionaries in Python or hash tables in other languages. Maps allow **fast lookups, additions, and deletions**.

6.2.1 Declaring and Initializing a Map

Maps are created using make() or with a literal.

Using make()

```go
CopyEdit
user := make(map[string]int)  // Creates an empty map
```

Using a Map Literal

```go
CopyEdit
ages := map[string]int{
    "Alice": 25,
    "Bob":   30,
}
fmt.Println(ages)  // Output: map[Alice:25 Bob:30]
```

6.2.2 Adding and Updating Key-Value Pairs

Maps store data in {key: value} format.

Example: Adding Entries

```go
CopyEdit
user["John"] = 40
user["Doe"] = 35
fmt.Println(user)  // Output: map[John:40 Doe:35]
```

Example: Updating Values

go
CopyEdit
```go
user["John"] = 50
fmt.Println(user["John"]) // Output: 50
```

6.2.3 Retrieving Values from a Map

To **fetch a value**, provide the key.

go
CopyEdit
```go
age := ages["Alice"]
fmt.Println("Alice's age:", age)
```

✔ **If the key does not exist, Go returns the zero value (e.g., 0 for integers).**

6.2.4 Checking If a Key Exists

Use the **comma-ok idiom** to check if a key is present.

go
CopyEdit
```go
value, exists := ages["Charlie"]
if exists {
    fmt.Println("Charlie's age:", value)
} else {
    fmt.Println("Charlie is not in the map.")
}
```

✔ **Prevents accessing non-existent keys.**

6.2.5 Deleting a Key from a Map

Use delete() to remove a key.

go
CopyEdit
```
delete(ages, "Bob")
fmt.Println(ages) // Output: map[Alice:25]
```

6.2.6 Iterating Over a Map

Use range to loop through key-value pairs.

go
CopyEdit
```
for key, value := range ages {
    fmt.Printf("%s is %d years old\n", key, value)
}
```

6.2.7 When to Use Maps vs. Slices

✔ Use maps when you need fast lookups based on a key.
✔ Use slices when order matters or when storing lists of elements.

✔ Arrays and slices store ordered data, while maps provide fast key-value lookups.
✔ Slices are preferred over arrays due to their flexibility.
✔ Maps are great for fast, unordered key-value storage

6.3 Strings in Go and String Manipulation

Strings in Go are immutable, meaning their contents cannot be modified after creation. Go provides built-in support for string manipulation, including concatenation, substring extraction, searching, and formatting.

6.3.1 Declaring Strings in Go

Strings in Go are enclosed in double quotes (").

go

CopyEdit

```go
var message string = "Hello, Go!"

fmt.Println(message)  // Output: Hello, Go!
```

String Shorthand Declaration

go

CopyEdit

```go
greeting := "Welcome to Golang"

fmt.Println(greeting)
```

Multi-line Strings

Use backticks (`) to create raw string literals.

go

CopyEdit

```go
note := `This is

a multi-line
```

string.`

fmt.Println(note)

✔ **Backticks (`) preserve line breaks and special characters.**

6.3.2 Concatenating Strings

Concatenation joins multiple strings together.

go

CopyEdit

```
first := "Hello"

second := "World"

full := first + ", " + second + "!"

fmt.Println(full)  // Output: Hello, World!
```

✔ **The + operator joins strings.**

6.3.3 Finding Substrings in a String

Use the strings.Contains() function to check if a string contains another string.

go

CopyEdit

```
import "strings"


text := "Golang is great"
```

```go
found := strings.Contains(text, "great")

fmt.Println(found)  // Output: true
```

✔ **Returns true if the substring exists.**

6.3.4 Extracting a Substring

There is no built-in substring function in Go, but slicing can be used.

go

CopyEdit

```go
sentence := "Programming"

sub := sentence[0:4]  // Extracts "Prog"

fmt.Println(sub)
```

✔ **Indexes start at 0, and slicing excludes the last index (4).**

6.3.5 Splitting a String

Use strings.Split() to divide a string into parts.

go

CopyEdit

```go
words := strings.Split("Go is fast", " ")

fmt.Println(words)  // Output: [Go is fast]
```

✔ Splits "Go is fast" into a slice of words.

6.3.6 Changing String Case

Go provides functions for converting string case.

go

CopyEdit

```
fmt.Println(strings.ToUpper("hello")) // Output: HELLO

fmt.Println(strings.ToLower("WORLD")) // Output: world
```

✔ Useful for case-insensitive comparisons.

6.3.7 Trimming Whitespace

Use strings.TrimSpace() to remove leading and trailing spaces.

go

CopyEdit

```
input := "   Golang   "

fmt.Println(strings.TrimSpace(input)) // Output: Golang
```

6.3.8 Replacing Parts of a String

Use strings.ReplaceAll() to replace parts of a string.

go

CopyEdit

original := "I love Java"

modified := strings.ReplaceAll(original, "Java", "Go")

fmt.Println(modified) // Output: I love Go

✔ Finds "Java" and replaces it with "Go".

6.4 Iterating Over Collections

Collections like arrays, slices, maps, and strings can be looped over using for and range.

6.4.1 Iterating Over an Array

go

CopyEdit

arr := [3]string{"Apple", "Banana", "Cherry"}

for i := 0; i < len(arr); i++ {

   fmt.Println(arr[i])

}

✔ Loops through an array using len().

6.4.2 Iterating Over a Slice Using range

go

CopyEdit

```
fruits := []string{"Mango", "Peach", "Grapes"}


for index, value := range fruits {
    fmt.Printf("Index: %d, Value: %s\n", index, value)
}
```

✔ **Returns both the index and value.**

✔ **Ignore the index using _:**

go

CopyEdit

```
for _, fruit := range fruits {
    fmt.Println(fruit)
}
```

6.4.3 Iterating Over a Map

go

CopyEdit

```
students := map[string]int{"Alice": 22, "Bob": 25}
```

```go
for name, age := range students {
    fmt.Printf("%s is %d years old\n", name, age)
}
```

✔ Maps return key-value pairs.

6.4.4 Iterating Over a String (Rune by Rune)

go

CopyEdit

```go
for _, char := range "Go" {
    fmt.Printf("%c\n", char)
}
```

✔ This prints:

nginx

CopyEdit

```
G
o
```

✔ Using range ensures correct iteration over Unicode characters.

6.5 Memory Efficiency in Collections

Efficient memory management is crucial when working with large datasets. Go provides several ways to optimize memory usage in collections.

6.5.1 Avoiding Unnecessary Slice Resizing

Slices dynamically grow, but frequent resizing is costly. Use make() to pre-allocate memory.

Inefficient Slice Expansion

go

CopyEdit

```go
var numbers []int

for i := 0; i < 1000; i++ {

    numbers = append(numbers, i) // Causes multiple memory allocations

}
```

🔺 append() **causes frequent memory reallocations.**

Optimized Slice Allocation

go

CopyEdit

```go
numbers := make([]int, 0, 1000) // Pre-allocate memory

for i := 0; i < 1000; i++ {

    numbers = append(numbers, i)

}
```

✔ Allocating capacity (1000) reduces reallocation overhead.

6.5.2 Using Pointers in Large Structs

If a struct is large, passing it by value is inefficient.

Inefficient Struct Passing (Creates Copies)

go

CopyEdit

```
type Student struct {
    name  string
    score int
}


func printStudent(s Student) {
    fmt.Println(s.name, s.score)
}
```

🔔 A copy of the struct is created when passing it to printStudent().

Optimized Struct Passing (Using Pointers)

go

CopyEdit

```
func printStudent(s *Student) { // Accepts a pointer
```

97

```go
    fmt.Println(s.name, s.score)
}


s := Student{"Alice", 90}

printStudent(&s) // Pass by reference
```

✔ Reduces memory usage for large structs.

6.5.3 Reducing Map Memory Overhead

Maps consume extra memory due to hash table storage. Deleting unused keys can reclaim memory.

Example: Removing Unused Map Keys

go

CopyEdit

```go
users := map[string]bool{"admin": true, "guest": false}

delete(users, "guest") // Free memory occupied by "guest"
```

✔ Reduces memory consumption when keys are no longer needed.

6.5.4 Using strings.Builder for Efficient String Concatenation

Concatenating strings using + is inefficient because Go creates a new string in memory every time.

Inefficient String Concatenation

go

CopyEdit

```
result := ""
for i := 0; i < 1000; i++ {
    result += "X"  // Creates a new string each iteration
}
```

🔔 Causes unnecessary memory allocation.

Optimized with strings.Builder

go

CopyEdit

```
import "strings"

var sb strings.Builder
for i := 0; i < 1000; i++ {
    sb.WriteString("X")
}
result := sb.String()
```

✔ strings.Builder **efficiently appends strings without extra allocations.**

✔ Strings are immutable but provide flexible manipulation functions.
✔ Efficient iteration over arrays, slices, maps, and strings improves performance.
✔ Using pre-allocated slices, pointers, and optimized map handling reduces memory overhead

Chapter 7: Structs and Interfaces

Go is not an object-oriented language in the traditional sense (like Java or Python), but it provides powerful mechanisms for **structuring data** and **attaching behavior** through **structs and methods**. Structs allow developers to create **custom data types**, and methods let them define **behavior** on those types.

7.1 Defining and Using Structs

A **struct** (short for **structure**) in Go is a **composite data type** that groups together multiple fields of different types under a single name. Structs are similar to **classes** in object-oriented programming but **do not support inheritance**.

7.1.1 Defining a Struct

A struct is declared using the type keyword followed by a **name** and a list of **fields** enclosed in curly braces {}.

Example: Defining a Struct

```go
CopyEdit
type Person struct {
    Name string
    Age  int
}
```

✔ **Person** is a new data type with two fields:

- Name of type string
- Age of type int

7.1.2 Creating and Initializing a Struct

There are several ways to **create** and **initialize** a struct.

1. Using a Struct Literal (Direct Initialization)

go
CopyEdit
```
p1 := Person{Name: "Alice", Age: 30}
fmt.Println(p1) // Output: {Alice 30}
```

✔ Fields are **explicitly initialized**.

2. Initializing with Default Values

go
CopyEdit
```
var p2 Person
fmt.Println(p2) // Output: { 0 }
```

✔ **Uninitialized fields** get Go's **zero values** ("" for strings, 0 for integers, false for booleans).

3. Partial Initialization

go
CopyEdit
```
p3 := Person{Name: "Bob"}
fmt.Println(p3) // Output: {Bob 0}
```

✔ Age **is set to 0 because it's not explicitly initialized.**

4. Using the new Keyword

go
CopyEdit
```
p4 := new(Person) // Returns a pointer to a struct
p4.Name = "Charlie"
p4.Age = 25
fmt.Println(*p4) // Output: {Charlie 25}
```

✔ new(Person) **creates a zero-initialized struct and returns a pointer to it.**

7.1.3 Accessing and Modifying Struct Fields

Struct fields are accessed using **dot notation (.)**.

Example: Modifying Struct Fields
go
CopyEdit
```
p1 := Person{Name: "Eve", Age: 40}
p1.Age = 41  // Modifying a field
fmt.Println(p1.Age)  // Output: 41
```

✔ **Struct values are mutable unless explicitly marked as** const.

7.1.4 Pointers to Structs

Structs can be passed **by reference** using pointers.

Example: Using a Pointer to Modify a Struct
go
CopyEdit
```
func updatePerson(p *Person) {
    p.Age += 1  // Modifies original struct
}

func main() {
    p := Person{Name: "David", Age: 29}
    updatePerson(&p)  // Pass pointer to function
    fmt.Println(p.Age)  // Output: 30
}
```

✔ **Passing by reference (*Person) ensures that changes persist outside the function.**
✔ **Without a pointer, Go passes a copy, and changes wouldn't affect the original struct.**

7.2 Methods and Structs (Object-Oriented Programming in Go)

Although Go doesn't have **classes**, it allows defining methods on **structs**, making it possible to implement **object-oriented principles**.

7.2.1 Defining Methods on a Struct

A **method** in Go is a function that is **associated with a struct**. Methods provide **behavior** for structs.

Example: Adding a Method to a Struct

go
CopyEdit

```go
type Person struct {
    Name string
    Age  int
}

// Method to display Person details
func (p Person) Display() {
    fmt.Printf("Name: %s, Age: %d\n", p.Name, p.Age)
}

func main() {
    p := Person{Name: "Alice", Age: 25}
    p.Display() // Output: Name: Alice, Age: 25
}
```

✔ **The method Display() is attached to Person.**
✔ **The receiver (p Person) binds the method to the struct.**

7.2.2 Methods with Pointers (Modifying Struct Fields)

By default, Go passes **struct values by copy**, so methods **cannot modify the original struct**. Use **pointers (*)** to modify struct fields inside methods.

Example: Updating Struct Fields via Method

go
CopyEdit

```go
type Account struct {
    Balance float64
}

// Method with pointer receiver to modify struct field
func (a *Account) Deposit(amount float64) {
    a.Balance += amount  // Modifies the original struct
}

func main() {
    acc := Account{Balance: 100.0}
    acc.Deposit(50.0)
    fmt.Println(acc.Balance)  // Output: 150.0
}
```

✔ Using a pointer receiver (*Account) allows modification of struct fields.
✔ Without *Account, Go would create a copy, and changes wouldn't persist.

7.2.3 Methods vs. Functions in Go

Feature	Method	Function
Association	Attached to a struct	Standalone
Call Syntax	`p.MethodName()`	`functionName(param)`
Receivers	Accepts struct instance	Accepts parameters

✔ Use methods when the function logically belongs to a struct.
✔ Use standalone functions for generic operations.

7.2.4 Struct Embedding (Composition in Go)

Go doesn't support **class inheritance**, but it allows **struct embedding** to create hierarchical relationships.

Example: Struct Embedding
go
CopyEdit

```go
type Employee struct {
    Name   string
    Salary float64
}

type Manager struct {
    Employee  // Embedding Employee struct
    TeamSize int
}

func main() {
    m := Manager{
        Employee: Employee{Name: "John", Salary: 80000},
        TeamSize: 10,
    }
    fmt.Println(m.Name, m.Salary, m.TeamSize)
}
```

✔ **Manager includes all fields from Employee.**
✔ **Allows code reuse without explicit inheritance.**

_____

7.2.5 Implementing Interfaces with Structs

Go uses **interfaces** to define behavior without enforcing strict inheritance.

106

Example: Implementing an Interface

go
CopyEdit

```go
type Shape interface {
    Area() float64
}

type Circle struct {
    Radius float64
}

// Implementing the interface
func (c Circle) Area() float64 {
    return 3.14 * c.Radius * c.Radius
}

func main() {
    c := Circle{Radius: 5}
    fmt.Println("Circle Area:", c.Area())
}
```

✔ Circle **implements** Shape **by defining the** Area() **method.**
✔ **Any type that implements** Area() **automatically satisfies** Shape**.**

✔ **Structs provide a way to define custom data types.**
✔ **Methods add behavior to structs, similar to object-oriented programming.**
✔ **Using pointers allows modifying struct fields inside methods.**
✔ **Struct embedding enables code reuse without inheritance.**
✔ **Interfaces define behavior for different struct types.**

7.3 Interfaces in Go (Dynamic Behavior in Static Typing)

Go is a **statically typed** language, meaning all variables and types are known at compile time. However, **interfaces** provide a way to achieve **dynamic behavior** while maintaining type safety.

An **interface** defines a set of methods that a type must implement. Unlike other languages, Go does not require explicit declarations that a type implements an interface—**if a type defines the methods required by an interface, it automatically satisfies that interface**.

7.3.1 Defining and Using an Interface

An interface in Go is declared using the type keyword and consists of **one or more method signatures**.

Example: Creating and Implementing an Interface

go
CopyEdit

```
package main

import "fmt"

// Define an interface
type Speaker interface {
    Speak() string
}

// Define a struct
type Person struct {
    Name string
}

// Implement the interface method
func (p Person) Speak() string {
    return "Hello, my name is " + p.Name
}
```

```go
func main() {
    var s Speaker  // Declare a variable of type Speaker interface
    s = Person{Name: "Alice"}  // Assign a struct that implements Speak()

    fmt.Println(s.Speak())  // Output: Hello, my name is Alice
}
```

✔ **The Person struct automatically satisfies the Speaker interface** because it implements the Speak() method.
✔ **Go does not require explicit declaration like implements or extends.**

7.3.2 Interfaces with Multiple Methods

An interface can have multiple methods that must all be implemented by a struct.

Example: A More Complex Interface
go
CopyEdit
```
type Animal interface {
    Speak() string
    Move() string
}

type Dog struct {
    Name string
}

func (d Dog) Speak() string {
    return "Woof!"
}

func (d Dog) Move() string {
    return "Runs on four legs"
}
```

```
func main() {
    var a Animal = Dog{Name: "Buddy"}
    fmt.Println(a.Speak()) // Output: Woof!
    fmt.Println(a.Move())  // Output: Runs on four legs
}
```

✔ **A type must implement all methods of an interface to satisfy it.**
✔ **Interfaces allow writing functions that accept multiple types with shared behavior.**

7.3.3 Empty Interfaces (interface{})

An **empty interface** (interface{}) can hold values of **any type**.

Example: Using interface{} for Dynamic Values
go
CopyEdit
```
func printValue(val interface{}) {
    fmt.Println(val)
}

func main() {
    printValue(42)         // Output: 42
    printValue("Go Lang")  // Output: Go Lang
    printValue(3.14)       // Output: 3.14
}
```

✔ **Useful for generic functions that handle multiple data types.**
✔ **Can be used in map[string]interface{} for flexible key-value storage.**

7.3.4 Type Assertions and Type Switches

Since interface{} can hold any value, **type assertions** and **type switches** allow retrieving the original type.

110

Example: Type Assertion

go
CopyEdit
```go
func describe(i interface{}) {
    val, ok := i.(string)  // Type assertion
    if ok {
        fmt.Println("This is a string:", val)
    } else {
        fmt.Println("Not a string")
    }
}

func main() {
    describe("Hello")  // Output: This is a string: Hello
    describe(123)      // Output: Not a string
}
```

✔ **i.(string) attempts to extract a string from the interface.**
✔ **ok is true if the assertion succeeds, false otherwise.**

Example: Type Switch

go
CopyEdit
```go
func checkType(i interface{}) {
    switch v := i.(type) {
    case int:
        fmt.Println("Integer:", v)
    case string:
        fmt.Println("String:", v)
    default:
        fmt.Println("Unknown type")
    }
}

func main() {
    checkType(100)       // Output: Integer: 100
    checkType("GoLang")  // Output: String: GoLang
```

```
    checkType(3.14)     // Output: Unknown type
}
```

✔ **Switching on type allows handling multiple types dynamically.**

7.3.5 Practical Use Cases of Interfaces

■ **Abstraction** – Functions operate on interfaces instead of concrete types.
■ **Polymorphism** – Different types can be treated the same way if they implement the same interface.
■ **Mocking in Testing** – Interfaces allow easy substitution of dependencies in unit tests.

Example: Interface for Database Operations

go
CopyEdit
```
type Database interface {
    Connect() string
}

type MySQL struct{}
func (m MySQL) Connect() string {
    return "Connected to MySQL"
}

type PostgreSQL struct{}
func (p PostgreSQL) Connect() string {
    return "Connected to PostgreSQL"
}

func getConnection(db Database) {
    fmt.Println(db.Connect())
}

func main() {
    getConnection(MySQL{})      // Output: Connected to MySQL
```

112

```
    getConnection(PostgreSQL{}) // Output: Connected to PostgreSQL
}
```

✔ **Allows switching databases without changing function logic.**

7.4 Composition Over Inheritance: Go's Unique Approach

Go **does not support classical inheritance** (as found in Java or C++). Instead, it promotes **composition**, which is a more flexible and maintainable way to **reuse code.**

7.4.1 Why Go Avoids Inheritance

🚫 **No subclassing** (extends) – No parent-child relationships.
🚫 **No method overriding** – Methods are not inherited.
🚫 **No deep class hierarchies** – No complicated dependencies.

Instead, Go promotes **composition**, where structs are built by **combining other structs**.

7.4.2 Struct Embedding (Composition in Go)

Instead of inheritance, Go allows **struct embedding**, where one struct includes another.

Example: Struct Embedding
go
CopyEdit
```
type Engine struct {
    Horsepower int
}

type Car struct {
    Brand  string
    Engine  // Embedded struct
}

func main() {
```

113

```go
	c := Car{Brand: "Toyota", Engine: Engine{Horsepower: 200}}
	fmt.Println(c.Brand)       // Output: Toyota
	fmt.Println(c.Horsepower)  // Output: 200
}
```

✔ **Car contains all fields of Engine without explicit inheritance.**
✔ **c.Horsepower directly accesses Engine's field.**

7.4.3 Overriding Embedded Struct Methods

Embedded structs can **override methods** by defining them explicitly in the outer struct.

Example: Overriding an Embedded Method
go
CopyEdit
```go
type Animal struct{}

func (a Animal) Speak() string {
	return "Some sound"
}

type Dog struct {
	Animal
}

func (d Dog) Speak() string {  // Overrides Animal's Speak()
	return "Woof!"
}

func main() {
	d := Dog{}
	fmt.Println(d.Speak())  // Output: Woof!
}
```

✔ **Go allows overriding by defining a new method in the embedding struct.**

114

7.4.4 Composition with Interfaces

Composition can also be done **using interfaces** instead of direct struct embedding.

Example: Interface-Based Composition
go
CopyEdit
```go
type Flyer interface {
    Fly() string
}

type Bird struct{}

func (b Bird) Fly() string {
    return "Bird is flying"
}

type Airplane struct{}

func (a Airplane) Fly() string {
    return "Airplane is flying"
}

func showFlying(f Flyer) {
    fmt.Println(f.Fly())
}

func main() {
    showFlying(Bird{})     // Output: Bird is flying
    showFlying(Airplane{}) // Output: Airplane is flying
}
```

✔ **Multiple types (Bird, Airplane) can implement the same behavior (Fly()).**

✔ Interfaces allow dynamic behavior in Go while keeping it statically typed.
✔ Composition via struct embedding is preferred over inheritance.
✔ Go's interface system allows flexible, decoupled designs.
✔ Type assertions and switches allow working with generic types efficiently

Chapter 8: Working with Files and JSON

Go provides built-in support for **file handling** and **JSON processing**, making it easy to work with structured data and persistent storage. This chapter covers how to **read and write files**, and how to **encode and decode JSON** in Go.

8.1 Reading and Writing to Files

The os and io/ioutil packages provide functions to handle **file operations** in Go. You can perform **reading, writing, and appending** to files with ease.

8.1.1 Writing to a File in Go

Go provides multiple ways to write data to a file, including **creating new files** and **appending to existing ones**.

Creating and Writing a New File

The os.Create() function creates a new file or **truncates** an existing file before writing.

```go
CopyEdit
package main

import (
    "fmt"
    "os"
)

func main() {
    file, err := os.Create("example.txt") // Create a file
    if err != nil {
        fmt.Println("Error creating file:", err)
        return
    }
```

```go
    defer file.Close() // Ensure the file is closed after function execution

    _, err = file.WriteString("Hello, Go!\n")
    if err != nil {
        fmt.Println("Error writing to file:", err)
    }
    fmt.Println("File written successfully")
}
```

✔ **Creates a new file (example.txt) and writes "Hello, Go!\n" to it.**
✔ **defer file.Close() ensures the file is closed when the function exits.**

Appending to an Existing File

To add new content to a file **without deleting existing data**, open it in **append mode**.

go
CopyEdit
```go
func main() {
    file, err := os.OpenFile("example.txt", os.O_APPEND|os.O_WRONLY, 0644)
    if err != nil {
        fmt.Println("Error opening file:", err)
        return
    }
    defer file.Close()

    _, err = file.WriteString("Appending new data...\n")
    if err != nil {
        fmt.Println("Error appending to file:", err)
    }
}
```

✔ **Opens example.txt in append mode (os.O_APPEND).**
✔ **Appends "Appending new data...\n" without erasing previous content.**

118

8.1.2 Reading from a File in Go

Reading files can be done using different approaches depending on the size and complexity of the data.

Reading an Entire File at Once

The os.ReadFile() function reads an entire file into memory.

```go
CopyEdit
package main

import (
    "fmt"
    "os"
)

func main() {
    data, err := os.ReadFile("example.txt")
    if err != nil {
        fmt.Println("Error reading file:", err)
        return
    }
    fmt.Println("File content:\n", string(data))
}
```

✔ Reads the entire file into memory and prints it.
✔ Best for small files, as large files may consume too much memory.

Reading a File Line by Line

For larger files, use bufio.Scanner to read **line by line**.

```go
CopyEdit
package main
```

```go
import (
    "bufio"
    "fmt"
    "os"
)

func main() {
    file, err := os.Open("example.txt")
    if err != nil {
        fmt.Println("Error opening file:", err)
        return
    }
    defer file.Close()

    scanner := bufio.NewScanner(file)
    for scanner.Scan() {
        fmt.Println(scanner.Text())  // Print each line
    }

    if err := scanner.Err(); err != nil {
        fmt.Println("Error reading file:", err)
    }
}
```

✔ **Efficient for large files as it reads one line at a time.**

8.1.3 Checking if a File Exists

Before reading or writing, you may need to check if a file **exists**.

go
CopyEdit
```go
func fileExists(filename string) bool {
    _, err := os.Stat(filename)
    return !os.IsNotExist(err)
```

```
}

func main() {
  if fileExists("example.txt") {
    fmt.Println("File exists!")
  } else {
    fmt.Println("File does not exist!")
  }
}
```

✔ Uses os.Stat() to check file existence.

8.1.4 Deleting a File

Use os.Remove() to delete a file.

go
CopyEdit
```
func main() {
  err := os.Remove("example.txt")
  if err != nil {
    fmt.Println("Error deleting file:", err)
  } else {
    fmt.Println("File deleted successfully")
  }
}
```

✔ Deletes example.txt permanently.

8.2 Working with JSON in Go

Go's encoding/json package provides built-in support for **encoding and decoding JSON data**.

121

8.2.1 Encoding (Converting Structs to JSON)

JSON encoding converts **Go structs** into JSON format.

Example: Encoding a Struct to JSON

go
CopyEdit

```
package main

import (
    "encoding/json"
    "fmt"
)

type User struct {
    Name  string `json:"name"`
    Age   int    `json:"age"`
    Email string `json:"email"`
}

func main() {
    user := User{Name: "Alice", Age: 25, Email: "alice@example.com"}

    jsonData, err := json.Marshal(user) // Convert struct to JSON
    if err != nil {
        fmt.Println("Error encoding JSON:", err)
        return
    }
    fmt.Println(string(jsonData)) // Output:
{"name":"Alice","age":25,"email":"alice@example.com"}
}
```

✔ **json:"name" ensures field names use lowercase keys in JSON.**
✔ **json.Marshal() converts the struct to a JSON byte slice.**

8.2.2 Decoding (Parsing JSON into Structs)

To convert JSON back into a struct, use json.Unmarshal().

Example: Decoding JSON into a Struct

go
CopyEdit

```
package main

import (
  "encoding/json"
  "fmt"
)

func main() {
  jsonString := `{"name":"Alice","age":25,"email":"alice@example.com"}`

  var user User
  err := json.Unmarshal([]byte(jsonString), &user) // Convert JSON to struct
  if err != nil {
    fmt.Println("Error decoding JSON:", err)
    return
  }
  fmt.Println(user.Name, user.Age, user.Email) // Output: Alice 25 alice@example.com
}
```

✔ json.Unmarshal() **populates the struct fields from JSON.**
✔ **Pass the struct by reference (&user) to modify its contents.**

8.2.3 Handling JSON Arrays

Go can encode and decode **JSON arrays** as slices.

Example: Encoding a Slice of Structs

go
CopyEdit

```go
users := []User{
    {Name: "Alice", Age: 25, Email: "alice@example.com"},
    {Name: "Bob", Age: 30, Email: "bob@example.com"},
}

jsonData, _ := json.Marshal(users)
fmt.Println(string(jsonData))
// Output:
[{"name":"Alice","age":25,"email":"alice@example.com"},{"name":"Bob","age":30,"email":"bob@example.com"}]
```

Example: Decoding JSON Arrays into a Slice

go
CopyEdit
```go
jsonString :=
`[{"name":"Alice","age":25,"email":"alice@example.com"},{"name":"Bob","age":30,"email":"bob@example.com"}]`

var users []User
json.Unmarshal([]byte(jsonString), &users)

for _, user := range users {
    fmt.Println(user.Name, user.Age)
}
```

✔ Parses a JSON array into a slice of User structs.

8.2.4 Writing JSON to a File

go
CopyEdit
```go
file, _ := os.Create("users.json")
defer file.Close()

json.NewEncoder(file).Encode(users)
```

124

✔ Writes JSON data directly to a file.

8.2.5 Reading JSON from a File

go
CopyEdit

```
file, _ := os.Open("users.json")
defer file.Close()

var users []User
json.NewDecoder(file).Decode(&users)
fmt.Println(users)
```

✔ Reads JSON directly from a file into a Go struct.

✔ Go provides built-in file handling with os and bufio for reading and writing files.
✔ JSON encoding and decoding is done using encoding/json.
✔ Use json.Unmarshal() to parse JSON into structs and json.Marshal() to encode structs into JSON.

8.3 Encoding and Decoding Data

Encoding and decoding are essential when working with structured data, allowing conversion between different formats like JSON, XML, and binary. Go provides the encoding package, which includes encoding/json, encoding/xml, and encoding/gob.

8.3.1 JSON Encoding and Decoding

Go's encoding/json **package is commonly used for converting Go structs to JSON (encoding) and parsing JSON into Go structs (decoding).**

Example: Encoding a Struct into JSON

go

CopyEdit

```go
package main

import (
    "encoding/json"
    "fmt"
)

type Product struct {
    Name  string `json:"name"`
    Price float64 `json:"price"`
}

func main() {
    product := Product{Name: "Laptop", Price: 1200.50}

    jsonData, err := json.Marshal(product)  // Convert struct to JSON
```

```go
    if err != nil {

        fmt.Println("Error encoding JSON:", err)

        return

    }

    fmt.Println(string(jsonData))  // Output: {"name":"Laptop","price":1200.5}

}
```

✔ json.Marshal() **converts the struct into a JSON-formatted byte slice.**
✔ **The struct fields are tagged with** json:"name"**, so field names in JSON match expectations.**

Example: Decoding JSON into a Struct

go

CopyEdit

```go
package main

import (

    "encoding/json"

    "fmt"

)

func main() {

    jsonString := `{"name":"Laptop","price":1200.5}`
```

```go
    var product Product
    err := json.Unmarshal([]byte(jsonString), &product)  // Convert JSON to struct
    if err != nil {
        fmt.Println("Error decoding JSON:", err)
        return
    }
    fmt.Println(product.Name, product.Price)  // Output: Laptop 1200.5
}
```

✔ json.Unmarshal() **parses JSON and maps it to the struct fields.**
✔ **The** &product **ensures that changes persist outside the function.**

8.3.2 Encoding and Decoding XML

Go's encoding/xml **package works similarly to** encoding/json **but is used for XML data.**

Example: Encoding Structs to XML

go

CopyEdit

```go
package main

import (
    "encoding/xml"
    "fmt"
```

```go
)

type Employee struct {
    XMLName xml.Name `xml:"employee"`
    ID      int      `xml:"id"`
    Name    string   `xml:"name"`
    Role    string   `xml:"role"`
}

func main() {
    emp := Employee{ID: 101, Name: "John Doe", Role: "Developer"}

    xmlData, err := xml.MarshalIndent(emp, "", "  ") // Convert struct to XML
    if err != nil {
        fmt.Println("Error encoding XML:", err)
        return
    }
    fmt.Println(string(xmlData))
}
```

✔ xml.MarshalIndent() **produces a well-formatted XML string.**
✔ **XML tags (**xml:"id"**) ensure proper field names in the output.**

Example: Decoding XML into a Struct

go

CopyEdit

```go
package main

import (
    "encoding/xml"
    "fmt"
)

func main() {
    xmlString := `<employee><id>101</id><name>John Doe</name><role>Developer</role></employee>`

    var emp Employee
    err := xml.Unmarshal([]byte(xmlString), &emp) // Convert XML to struct
    if err != nil {
        fmt.Println("Error decoding XML:", err)
        return
    }
    fmt.Println(emp.Name, emp.Role) // Output: John Doe Developer
}
```

✔ xml.Unmarshal() **maps XML fields to struct properties.**

8.3.3 Encoding and Decoding Binary Data (gob)

Go's encoding/gob **package is used for binary serialization, making it faster than JSON and XML.**

Example: Encoding Data Using gob

go

CopyEdit

```go
package main

import (
    "bytes"
    "encoding/gob"
    "fmt"
)

type User struct {
    Name  string
    Email string
}
```

```go
func main() {
    var buf bytes.Buffer
    encoder := gob.NewEncoder(&buf)

    user := User{Name: "Alice", Email: "alice@example.com"}
    err := encoder.Encode(user)  // Convert struct to binary
    if err != nil {
        fmt.Println("Error encoding:", err)
        return
    }
    fmt.Println("Binary data:", buf.Bytes())
}
```

✔ **Efficient storage format, ideal for inter-process communication (IPC).**

Example: Decoding gob Binary Data

go

CopyEdit

```go
func main() {
    var buf bytes.Buffer
    encoder := gob.NewEncoder(&buf)
    decoder := gob.NewDecoder(&buf)
```

```go
user := User{Name: "Alice", Email: "alice@example.com"}

encoder.Encode(user)  // Encode struct to binary


var decodedUser User

err := decoder.Decode(&decodedUser)  // Decode binary data back to struct

if err != nil {

    fmt.Println("Error decoding:", err)

    return

}

    fmt.Println(decodedUser.Name, decodedUser.Email)  // Output: Alice
alice@example.com

}
```

✔ **Efficient for transmitting structured data between Go applications.**

8.4 Handling File Errors Gracefully

Error handling is critical when working with files to ensure robustness and prevent crashes.

8.4.1 Handling File Not Found Errors

Trying to open a non-existent file will cause an error.

go

CopyEdit

```go
package main

import (
    "fmt"
    "os"
)

func main() {
    _, err := os.Open("missing_file.txt")
    if err != nil {
        if os.IsNotExist(err) {
            fmt.Println("File does not exist!")
        } else {
            fmt.Println("Error opening file:", err)
        }
    }
}
```

✔ os.IsNotExist(err) **checks if the error is due to a missing file.**

8.4.2 Gracefully Handling File Read Errors

Errors can occur while reading large files. Always check for errors inside loops.

go

CopyEdit

```go
func readFile(filename string) {
    file, err := os.Open(filename)
    if err != nil {
        fmt.Println("Error opening file:", err)
        return
    }
    defer file.Close()

    scanner := bufio.NewScanner(file)
    for scanner.Scan() {
        fmt.Println(scanner.Text())
    }

    if err := scanner.Err(); err != nil {
        fmt.Println("Error reading file:", err)
    }
}
```

✔ Handles both opening and reading errors properly.

8.4.3 Handling File Writing Errors

Ensure that write operations check for errors.

go

CopyEdit

```go
func writeToFile(filename string, data string) {
    file, err := os.Create(filename)
    if err != nil {
        fmt.Println("Error creating file:", err)
        return
    }
    defer file.Close()

    _, err = file.WriteString(data)
    if err != nil {
        fmt.Println("Error writing to file:", err)
    } else {
        fmt.Println("Data written successfully")
    }
}
```

✔ Prevents incomplete file writes due to errors.

8.4.4 Recovering from File Panics Using recover()

A function might panic if an unexpected file operation fails. Use recover() **to prevent crashes.**

go

CopyEdit

```go
func safeFileOperation() {

    defer func() {

        if r := recover(); r != nil {

            fmt.Println("Recovered from panic:", r)

        }

    }()


    file, err := os.Open("non_existent.txt")

    if err != nil {

        panic("Critical file missing!")  // Panic if file not found

    }

    defer file.Close()

}
```

✔ Ensures the program does not crash due to missing files.

✔ Go supports encoding and decoding JSON, XML, and binary (gob) formats.
✔ Use os, bufio, and ioutil for robust file operations.
✔ Always check for errors when working with files and recover from panics if necessary.

Chapter 9: Understanding Pointers and Memory Management

Memory management is a critical aspect of any programming language. Go provides **automatic memory management** via **garbage collection**, but **understanding pointers** allows developers to optimize performance, prevent unnecessary memory allocations, and avoid unintended data modifications.

This chapter will cover **pointers**, how they help in **efficient memory management**, and the differences between **passing variables by value vs. reference**.

9.1 Introduction to Pointers in Go

9.1.1 What Are Pointers?

A **pointer** is a variable that **stores the memory address** of another variable. Instead of holding a **direct value**, a pointer **references a memory location** where the actual value is stored.

Pointers allow **efficient data manipulation**, reducing memory overhead and preventing unnecessary copies of large data structures.

9.1.2 Declaring and Using Pointers

1. Declaring a Pointer

A pointer is declared using the * symbol.

```go
CopyEdit
var ptr *int  // Declares a pointer to an integer
```

✔ The *int type indicates a pointer to an integer.

2. Assigning a Memory Address to a Pointer

Use the **address-of operator (&)** to obtain the memory address of a variable.

go
CopyEdit
```
num := 10
ptr := &num  // Stores the address of num in ptr
fmt.Println("Address of num:", ptr)
fmt.Println("Value of num using pointer:", *ptr) // Dereferencing
```

✔ **ptr = &num stores the memory address of num in ptr.**
✔ ***ptr dereferences the pointer, retrieving the value stored at the memory address.**

---

3. Dereferencing a Pointer

Dereferencing a pointer means **accessing the value stored at the memory location**.

go
CopyEdit
```
var x int = 42
var p *int = &x  // Pointer stores the address of x

fmt.Println("Value of x:", *p)  // Output: 42
*p = 100                  // Modifies x via pointer
fmt.Println("New value of x:", x)  // Output: 100
```

✔ **Changing *p also modifies x since p points to x's memory.**

9.1.3 The nil Pointer

A pointer that does not point to any memory address is called a **nil pointer**.

go
CopyEdit
```
var ptr *int
```

140

```go
fmt.Println(ptr)  // Output: <nil>
```

✔ **Dereferencing a nil pointer (*ptr) causes a runtime error (panic).**

9.1.4 Creating Pointers Using new

Go provides the new function to allocate memory for a variable and return a pointer to it.

go
CopyEdit
```go
ptr := new(int)  // Creates an integer pointer
fmt.Println(*ptr)  // Output: 0 (default zero value)
*ptr = 25
fmt.Println(*ptr)  // Output: 25
```

✔ **new(int) returns a pointer to a zero-initialized integer.**

9.1.5 Using Struct Pointers

Pointers are widely used with structs to avoid copying large data structures.

go
CopyEdit
```go
type Person struct {
    Name string
    Age  int
}

func main() {
    p := &Person{Name: "Alice", Age: 30}  // Pointer to struct
    fmt.Println(p.Name)  // Output: Alice
}
```

✔ **p is a pointer to a** Person **struct.**
✔ **Struct fields can be accessed using** p.Name **(Go automatically dereferences p).**

9.2 Passing Variables by Value vs. Reference

In Go, function parameters are passed in two ways:

1. **By value** (default) → A copy of the variable is passed.
2. **By reference** (using pointers) → A memory address is passed, allowing modifications.

9.2.1 Passing by Value

By default, Go passes function arguments **by value**, meaning a **copy** of the variable is made.

Example: Passing by Value

go
CopyEdit

```
func changeValue(num int) {
    num = 20  // Changes only the local copy
}

func main() {
    x := 10
    changeValue(x)
    fmt.Println(x)  // Output: 10 (unchanged)
}
```

✔ **Changes made inside the function do not affect the original variable.**
✔ **This can lead to unnecessary memory usage when dealing with large data structures.**

9.2.2 Passing by Reference (Using Pointers)

To modify a variable inside a function, pass a **pointer** instead of a copy.

Example: Passing by Reference

go
CopyEdit

```
func changeValue(num *int) {
    *num = 20  // Modifies original variable
}

func main() {
    x := 10
    changeValue(&x) // Pass address of x
    fmt.Println(x) // Output: 20 (modified)
}
```

✔ **The function now modifies the original value because it receives a pointer (*int).**

9.2.3 Performance Comparison

Passing By	Memory Usage	Modification Allowed?	Use Case
Value	Creates a copy	No	Small data types, simple functions
Reference	Uses same memory	Yes	Large structs, shared data modifications

✔ **Use pointers when modifying large structs to avoid excessive memory usage.**
✔ **Use value-passing for small data types like integers, booleans, and floats.**

9.2.4 Using Pointers to Modify Structs

Structs are **copied** when passed by value. To modify struct fields inside a function, pass a **pointer**.

Example: Struct Modification with Pointers

go
CopyEdit
```
type Account struct {
    Balance float64
}

func deposit(a *Account, amount float64) {
    a.Balance += amount
}

func main() {
    acc := Account{Balance: 1000}
    deposit(&acc, 500)  // Passing struct pointer
    fmt.Println("Updated Balance:", acc.Balance)  // Output: 1500
}
```

✔ **Avoids unnecessary copying and allows direct modification.**

9.2.5 Returning Pointers from Functions

Functions can return **pointers** to allow efficient memory usage.

Example: Returning a Pointer

go
CopyEdit
```
func newPerson(name string, age int) *Person {
    return &Person{Name: name, Age: age}  // Returns struct pointer
}

func main() {
    p := newPerson("Bob", 35)
    fmt.Println(p.Name, p.Age)  // Output: Bob 35
}
```

✔ Returning pointers prevents unnecessary copies of large structs.

✔ Pointers allow direct memory access, reducing unnecessary copying.
✔ Dereferencing (*) retrieves values from pointers.
✔ Passing by reference modifies original data, improving efficiency.
✔ Use pointers for large data structures to optimize memory usage.

9.3 Managing Memory Efficiently in Go

Go is a garbage-collected language, meaning it automatically manages memory allocation and deallocation. However, developers can write efficient Go programs by understanding how Go's memory management works and applying best practices to optimize performance.

This section covers how Go manages memory, the differences between heap and stack memory, and techniques for efficient memory usage.

9.3.1 Understanding Go's Memory Management

Go's runtime automatically handles memory allocation and garbage collection, reducing the need for manual memory management (like in C or C++). However, understanding how memory is allocated and freed helps avoid unnecessary allocations, memory leaks, and performance bottlenecks.

Heap vs. Stack Memory in Go

Go's memory model consists of stack and heap memory:

Memory Type	Description	Usage in Go
Stack	Fast, managed memory for function calls and local variables	Used for local variables within a function
Heap	Slower but larger memory space for dynamically allocated variables	Used when variables outlive the function scope (e.g., struct pointers)

✔ Stack memory is automatically freed when a function returns.
✔ Heap memory is managed by the garbage collector (GC).

9.3.2 Avoiding Unnecessary Heap Allocations

Heap allocations cause garbage collection overhead, so optimizing stack memory usage improves performance.

Example: Using Stack Memory (Efficient)

go

CopyEdit

```go
func createPerson() Person {  // Returns a struct (allocated on stack)

    return Person{Name: "Alice", Age: 30}

}


func main() {

    p := createPerson()  // Efficient, no heap allocation

    fmt.Println(p.Name)

}
```

✔ Struct Person is allocated on the stack and automatically freed when the function returns.

Example: Using Heap Memory (Less Efficient)

go

CopyEdit

```go
func createPersonPointer() *Person {  // Returns a pointer (allocated on heap)
    return &Person{Name: "Alice", Age: 30}
}


func main() {
    p := createPersonPointer()  // Stored on heap, managed by GC
    fmt.Println(p.Name)
}
```

✔ Using &Person{} forces heap allocation, making garbage collection necessary.
✔ Use heap allocation only if the struct needs to persist beyond function scope.

9.3.3 Reducing Garbage Collection Overhead

Go's garbage collector (GC) automatically frees unused memory. However, excessive GC cycles can impact performance.

■ Best Practices to Reduce GC Overhead

✔ **Minimize Heap Allocations** – Prefer value types (struct) over pointers when possible.
✔ **Use Object Pooling** – Reuse allocated objects instead of repeatedly creating new ones.
✔ **Optimize Slice Capacity** – Preallocate slice capacity to avoid unnecessary reallocation.

9.3.4 Using Object Pooling to Reuse Memory

Go's sync.Pool helps reuse objects instead of creating and discarding them repeatedly.

Example: Object Pooling with sync.Pool

go

CopyEdit

```go
package main

import (
    "fmt"
    "sync"
)

var personPool = sync.Pool{
    New: func() interface{} {
```

```go
        return &Person{}
    },
}

type Person struct {
    Name string
}

func main() {
    p1 := personPool.Get().(*Person) // Get a Person from pool
    p1.Name = "Alice"

    fmt.Println(p1.Name) // Output: Alice

    personPool.Put(p1) // Return to pool for reuse

    p2 := personPool.Get().(*Person) // Get another Person
    fmt.Println(p2.Name) // Output: Alice (reused object)
}
```

✔ **Reuses allocated memory instead of creating new objects, reducing GC pressure.**

9.3.5 Optimizing Slice and Map Memory Usage

Slices and maps dynamically grow, but frequent reallocation can hurt performance.

Preallocating Slice Capacity

go

CopyEdit

```
nums := make([]int, 0, 1000) // Preallocates memory for 1000 elements
for i := 0; i < 1000; i++ {
    nums = append(nums, i)
}
```

✔ Preallocating prevents unnecessary memory reallocation.

Using delete() to Free Map Memory

go

CopyEdit

```
users := map[string]string{"Alice": "Engineer", "Bob": "Doctor"}
delete(users, "Bob") // Free memory occupied by "Bob"
```

✔ Removing unused map entries helps free memory.

9.3.6 Avoiding Memory Leaks in Go

Go automatically manages memory, but incorrect usage can still cause memory leaks.

Common Memory Leak Causes

🔒 Retaining Unused Pointers – Holding references to objects no longer needed.
🔒 Infinite Goroutines – Goroutines that never exit, keeping memory occupied.

Example: Preventing Goroutine Leaks

go

CopyEdit

```go
func startWorker(stop chan bool) {
    for {
        select {
        case <-stop:
            fmt.Println("Stopping worker")
            return
        default:
            // Worker logic here...
        }
    }
}


func main() {
    stop := make(chan bool)
    go startWorker(stop) // Starts goroutine
```

```go
    // Stop the worker after some time

    stop <- true

}
```

✔ Using `stop <- true` **ensures goroutine exits properly.**

9.3.7 Monitoring Memory Usage in Go

Use Go's built-in `runtime` **package to track memory usage and optimize performance.**

Example: Printing Memory Statistics

go

CopyEdit

```go
package main

import (
    "fmt"
    "runtime"
)

func main() {
    var memStats runtime.MemStats
    runtime.ReadMemStats(&memStats)
```

```
    fmt.Printf("Memory Allocated: %v KB\n", memStats.Alloc/1024)

    fmt.Printf("Heap Usage: %v KB\n", memStats.HeapAlloc/1024)

}
```

✔ Tracks memory consumption to identify excessive allocations.

✔ Go automatically manages memory, but efficient memory usage improves performance.
✔ Use stack allocations instead of heap when possible.
✔ Object pooling and preallocated slices/maps reduce GC overhead.
✔ Monitor memory usage to optimize application performance

Chapter 10: Concurrency in Go

Concurrency is one of Go's most powerful features, enabling efficient execution of multiple tasks **without blocking** program execution. Go achieves concurrency through **goroutines** and **channels**, making it easier to build scalable, high-performance applications.

This chapter covers **goroutines**, how they differ from traditional threads, and how **channels** enable safe communication between them.

10.1 Introduction to Goroutines

A **goroutine** is a **lightweight thread** managed by the Go runtime. Unlike traditional OS threads, goroutines are **more efficient**, allowing thousands (or even millions) to run concurrently.

10.1.1 What is a Goroutine?

A **goroutine** is a function that runs **independently** in the background, separate from the main program.

Example: Creating a Goroutine

go
CopyEdit

```
package main

import (
    "fmt"
    "time"
)

func printMessage() {
    fmt.Println("Hello from goroutine!")
}
```

```
func main() {
    go printMessage() // Run function in a separate goroutine
    time.Sleep(time.Second) // Allow time for goroutine to execute
}
```

✔ **go printMessage() starts printMessage() as a goroutine.**
✔ **Without time.Sleep, the main function may exit before the goroutine runs.**

10.1.2 Goroutines vs. Traditional Threads

Feature	Goroutines	Traditional Threads
Memory Usage	Uses only a few KB	Uses several MB
Performance	Efficient, runs thousands concurrently	Limited due to OS overhead
Scheduling	Managed by Go runtime	Managed by OS
Creation Time	Extremely fast	Slower

✔ **Goroutines make Go highly efficient for concurrent programming.**

10.1.3 Running Multiple Goroutines

Goroutines run **independently**, allowing multiple tasks to execute at the same time.

Example: Running Multiple Goroutines
go
CopyEdit
```
func task(name string) {
    for i := 0; i < 3; i++ {
        fmt.Println(name, "running iteration", i)
        time.Sleep(time.Millisecond * 500)
    }
}

func main() {
    go task("Task 1")
    go task("Task 2")
```

```
    time.Sleep(time.Second * 2)
}
```

✔ Both Task 1 and Task 2 **run concurrently.**
✔ **Output order may vary due to concurrent execution.**

10.1.4 The Problem of Goroutine Execution Timing

Since the **main function exits quickly,** some goroutines might not complete execution.

🔺 **Example: Missing Goroutine Execution**

go
CopyEdit
```
go fmt.Println("This may not print!")  // Goroutine runs asynchronously
```

✔ **The main function may exit before the goroutine executes.**

Solution: Using time.Sleep() **(Temporary Fix)**

go
CopyEdit
```
go fmt.Println("Hello from goroutine!")
time.Sleep(time.Second)  // Gives time for goroutine to run
```

✔ **Avoid using** time.Sleep **as a permanent solution.**

■ **Best Practice:** Use **channels** to synchronize goroutines properly.

10.2 Using Channels for Safe Communication

Goroutines run **independently,** but they need a way to **communicate** safely. Go provides **channels** to enable safe, synchronized data sharing between goroutines.

10.2.1 What is a Channel?

A **channel** is a **typed conduit** that allows goroutines to send and receive data safely.

Declaring a Channel

go
CopyEdit

```go
var ch chan int  // Declares a channel for integers
```

✔ **Channels must be initialized before use.**

Creating a Channel

go
CopyEdit

```go
ch := make(chan int)  // Creates an integer channel
```

✔ **make(chan int) initializes an unbuffered channel.**

10.2.2 Sending and Receiving Data with Channels

Channels enable **synchronous communication** between goroutines.

Example: Basic Channel Usage

go
CopyEdit

```go
package main

import "fmt"

func sendData(ch chan string) {
    ch <- "Hello from goroutine!"  // Send data into channel
}

func main() {
    ch := make(chan string)
    go sendData(ch)
```

```
msg := <-ch  // Receive data from channel
fmt.Println(msg)  // Output: Hello from goroutine!
}
```

✔ **ch <- "Hello" sends data into the channel.**
✔ **msg := <-ch receives data from the channel.**
✔ **Without a receiver, a send operation blocks indefinitely.**

10.2.3 Buffered vs. Unbuffered Channels

Channel Type	Description	Blocking Behavior
Unbuffered	Direct communication, requires sender and receiver	Blocks until receiver reads
Buffered	Holds limited data before blocking	Blocks when buffer is full

Creating a Buffered Channel

go
CopyEdit
```
ch := make(chan int, 3)  // Buffered channel with capacity 3
```

Example: Using a Buffered Channel

go
CopyEdit
```
func main() {
    ch := make(chan string, 2)  // Buffer size 2
    ch <- "First"
    ch <- "Second"

    fmt.Println(<-ch)  // Output: First
    fmt.Println(<-ch)  // Output: Second
}
```

✔ **Buffered channels allow sending data without an immediate receiver.**
✔ **Blocks only when the buffer is full.**

10.2.4 Closing a Channel

Channels should be **closed** when no more data will be sent.

Example: Closing a Channel

go
CopyEdit

```
func main() {
   ch := make(chan int, 2)
   ch <- 10
   ch <- 20
   close(ch)

   for num := range ch {
      fmt.Println(num)  // Output: 10, 20
   }
}
```

✔ **Use close(ch) to signal that no more values will be sent.**
✔ **range automatically stops reading when the channel is closed.**

🔔 **DO NOT close a channel multiple times (causes panic).**

10.2.5 Using select for Multiple Channels

Go's select statement enables **waiting on multiple channels** simultaneously.

Example: Handling Multiple Channels with select

go
CopyEdit

```
func main() {
   ch1 := make(chan string)
```

```go
ch2 := make(chan string)

go func() {
    time.Sleep(time.Second)
    ch1 <- "Message from channel 1"
}()

go func() {
    time.Sleep(time.Second * 2)
    ch2 <- "Message from channel 2"
}()

select {
case msg1 := <-ch1:
    fmt.Println(msg1)
case msg2 := <-ch2:
    fmt.Println(msg2)
}
}
```

✔ **Whichever channel receives data first gets executed.**
✔ **Prevents blocking while waiting for multiple goroutines.**

10.2.6 Preventing Deadlocks with Channels

A **deadlock** occurs when all goroutines are waiting, and no further execution can proceed.

🔔 Example: Deadlock Situation

go
CopyEdit
```go
ch := make(chan int)
ch <- 5  // Blocks indefinitely because no receiver exists
```

✔ To prevent deadlocks, always ensure a corresponding receiver.

✔ Goroutines enable lightweight concurrency without OS threads.
✔ Use channels for safe, synchronized communication.
✔ Buffered channels reduce blocking but should be sized carefully.
✔ Always close channels when no more data will be sent.
✔ Use select to manage multiple channels efficiently.

10.3 Buffered vs. Unbuffered Channels

10.3.1 Understanding Buffered and Unbuffered Channels

Go's channels come in two forms:

1. Unbuffered Channels – Used for direct communication between goroutines, where the sender blocks until the receiver reads the data.
2. Buffered Channels – Can hold multiple values before blocking, allowing the sender to continue execution without an immediate receiver.

10.3.2 Unbuffered Channels (Synchronous Communication)

An unbuffered channel ensures that a sender waits until a receiver reads the data.

Example: Unbuffered Channel

go

CopyEdit

```
package main


import (
```

```go
    "fmt"
)


func sendData(ch chan string) {
    ch <- "Hello from goroutine"  // Blocks until receiver reads
}


func main() {
    ch := make(chan string) // Unbuffered channel
    go sendData(ch)         // Start goroutine

    msg := <-ch // Waits for data from channel
    fmt.Println(msg) // Output: Hello from goroutine
}
```

✔ Sender blocks until data is received.
✔ Receiver waits if there is no available data.

🔔 Problem: If no goroutine is receiving, the program deadlocks because the sender is waiting indefinitely.

10.3.3 Buffered Channels (Asynchronous Communication)

A buffered channel allows sending multiple values without blocking until the buffer is full.

Example: Buffered Channel

go

CopyEdit

```go
func main() {
    ch := make(chan int, 3) // Buffer size of 3
    ch <- 1 // Doesn't block
    ch <- 2 // Doesn't block
    ch <- 3 // Doesn't block
    fmt.Println(<-ch) // Reads 1
    fmt.Println(<-ch) // Reads 2
    fmt.Println(<-ch) // Reads 3
}
```

✔ Sender does not block immediately.
✔ Only blocks when the buffer is full.

🔔 Problem: If no receiver exists, a full buffer blocks the sender indefinitely.

10.3.4 When to Use Buffered vs. Unbuffered Channels

Feature	Unbuffered Channel	Buffered Channel
Blocking Behavior	Sender waits until receiver reads	Sender waits only if buffer is full
Use Case	Real-time synchronization	Queue-like behavior
Performance	Lower latency	Higher throughput

■ Use unbuffered channels for real-time synchronization between goroutines.
■ Use buffered channels to queue tasks without blocking the sender immediately.

10.4 WaitGroups and Synchronization

Goroutines execute independently, but sometimes we need to wait for all goroutines to complete before continuing execution. Go's sync.WaitGroup helps manage this synchronization.

10.4.1 Using sync.WaitGroup to Wait for Goroutines

A WaitGroup waits for multiple goroutines to finish before continuing.

Example: Using WaitGroup

go

CopyEdit

```
package main

import (
    "fmt"
    "sync"
    "time"
)

func worker(id int, wg *sync.WaitGroup) {
```

```go
    defer wg.Done() // Marks this goroutine as finished
    fmt.Printf("Worker %d started\n", id)
    time.Sleep(time.Second) // Simulate work
    fmt.Printf("Worker %d finished\n", id)
}

func main() {
    var wg sync.WaitGroup

    for i := 1; i <= 3; i++ {
        wg.Add(1) // Add one goroutine to the WaitGroup
        go worker(i, &wg)
    }

    wg.Wait() // Wait for all goroutines to finish
    fmt.Println("All workers completed")
}
```

✔ wg.Add(1) **registers a new goroutine.**
✔ **Each goroutine calls** wg.Done() **to signal completion.**
✔ wg.Wait() **blocks execution until all goroutines finish.**

🔔 **Avoid calling** wg.Done() **more than once per goroutine, or it may cause panics.**

10.4.2 Ensuring Mutual Exclusion with sync.Mutex

Goroutines can access shared variables, leading to race conditions. A mutex ensures that only one goroutine modifies shared data at a time.

Example: Using sync.Mutex

go

CopyEdit

```go
package main

import (
    "fmt"
    "sync"
)

var counter int
var mutex sync.Mutex

func increment(wg *sync.WaitGroup) {
    defer wg.Done()
    mutex.Lock()   // Lock before modifying counter
    counter++
    mutex.Unlock() // Unlock after modification
}
```

```go
func main() {

    var wg sync.WaitGroup

    for i := 0; i < 5; i++ {

        wg.Add(1)

        go increment(&wg)

    }

    wg.Wait()

    fmt.Println("Final counter value:", counter)

}
```

✔ Ensures only one goroutine modifies counter at a time.
✔ Prevents race conditions when multiple goroutines access shared data.

🔒 Always Unlock() the mutex to prevent deadlocks.

10.5 Common Concurrency Pitfalls and How to Avoid Them

While Go makes concurrency easy, misusing goroutines and channels can lead to subtle bugs. Here are common pitfalls and best practices to avoid them.

10.5.1 Goroutine Leaks

Problem: A goroutine never exits, wasting memory indefinitely.

Example: Goroutine Leak

go

CopyEdit

```go
func startWorker() {
    ch := make(chan string)
    go func() {
        for msg := range ch {  // This goroutine never exits
            fmt.Println(msg)
        }
    }()
}


func main() {
    startWorker()
}
```

🔔 Goroutine remains running forever because ch is never closed.

Solution: Ensure Goroutines Can Exit

go

CopyEdit

```go
func startWorker(done chan bool) {
    go func() {
        for {
            select {
            case <-done:
                return  // Gracefully exit goroutine
            }
        }
    }()
}

func main() {
    done := make(chan bool)
    startWorker(done)
    done <- true  // Signal worker to stop
}
```

✔ **Goroutine exits when done receives a signal.**

10.5.2 Deadlocks

Problem: Goroutines block indefinitely, causing the program to hang.

Example: Deadlock (No Receiver)

go

CopyEdit

```
ch := make(chan int)

ch <- 10  // Blocks indefinitely because no receiver exists
```

Solution: Always Ensure a Receiver Exists

go

CopyEdit

```
go func() { ch <- 10 }()

fmt.Println(<-ch)  // Now there's a receiver
```

✔ A separate goroutine ensures the sender does not block.

10.5.3 Data Races

Problem: Multiple goroutines modify the same variable simultaneously, leading to unpredictable behavior.

Example: Data Race

go

CopyEdit

```go
var counter int

for i := 0; i < 5; i++ {

    go func() { counter++ }() // Multiple goroutines modifying counter

}

fmt.Println(counter)  // Unreliable output
```

Solution: Use sync.Mutex **or** sync/atomic

go

CopyEdit

```go
var counter int64
var wg sync.WaitGroup

for i := 0; i < 5; i++ {

    wg.Add(1)

    go func() {

        atomic.AddInt64(&counter, 1)  // Safe atomic increment

        wg.Done()

    }()

}
```

```
wg.Wait()

fmt.Println(counter)  // Consistent output
```

✔ Atomic operations ensure thread-safe modifications.

✔ Unbuffered channels enforce direct synchronization, while buffered channels provide queue-like behavior.
✔ Use sync.WaitGroup to wait for goroutines to complete.
✔ Use sync.Mutex or sync/atomic to prevent data races.
✔ Avoid goroutine leaks, deadlocks, and race conditions by following best practices.

Chapter 11: Web Development with Go

Go has become a **popular choice** for web development due to its **speed, simplicity, and powerful standard library**. With the built-in net/http package, developers can create **high-performance web applications** without needing third-party frameworks.

This chapter covers **setting up a web server**, handling HTTP requests and responses, and the fundamentals of **Go web development**.

11.1 Introduction to Web Development in Go

Go is well-suited for **backend web development**, offering:
✔ **Performance** – Faster than interpreted languages like Python and JavaScript.
✔ **Concurrency** – Goroutines allow efficient request handling.
✔ **Minimal Dependencies** – The net/http package provides all essentials.
✔ **Scalability** – Lightweight nature makes it great for microservices.

11.1.1 Key Components of Web Development in Go

Component	Description
net/http	Core package for handling HTTP requests and responses.
Routing	Determines how URLs map to handlers.
Middleware	Functions that process requests before reaching the final handler.
Templates	Used for rendering HTML responses.
JSON Handling	Encoding/decoding JSON data for APIs.

11.1.2 Why Use Go for Web Development?

✔ **Minimalist Standard Library** – Go provides built-in tools for HTTP handling, JSON parsing, and routing.
✔ **High Performance** – Go is compiled, leading to faster response times.
✔ **Easy Deployment** – Go produces a **single binary executable** with no runtime

dependencies.

✔ **Concurrency** – Goroutines enable efficient request handling.

✔ **Security** – Built-in protection against common vulnerabilities like buffer overflows.

11.1.3 Web Frameworks vs. Standard Library in Go

While Go's **standard library** is powerful, frameworks like **Gin**, **Echo**, and **Fiber** add more functionality.

Feature	Standard Library (net/http)	Go Web Frameworks (Gin, Echo, Fiber)
Routing	Basic with http.HandleFunc	Advanced routing and middleware support
Performance	High	Slightly lower due to extra features
Middleware	Requires manual setup	Built-in middleware support
Use Case	Simple, minimal applications	Feature-rich, complex applications

■ For simple APIs, net/http is sufficient.

■ For complex applications, a framework can help reduce boilerplate code.

11.2 Setting Up an HTTP Server with net/http

The net/http package allows developers to create a **lightweight HTTP server** quickly.

11.2.1 Starting a Basic HTTP Server

An HTTP server **listens for incoming requests** and responds based on predefined routes.

Example: Simple HTTP Server

```
go
CopyEdit
package main

import (
```

```go
    "fmt"
    "net/http"
)

// Handler function
func helloHandler(w http.ResponseWriter, r *http.Request) {
    fmt.Fprintln(w, "Hello, World!")
}

func main() {
    http.HandleFunc("/", helloHandler)  // Register route
    fmt.Println("Server started on :8080")
    http.ListenAndServe(":8080", nil)  // Start server on port 8080
}
```

✔ **Starts a server on** localhost:8080.
✔ **http.HandleFunc("/", helloHandler) registers a route.**
✔ **http.ListenAndServe(":8080", nil) listens for requests.**

11.2.2 Handling Different HTTP Methods

HTTP requests use different **methods** (GET, POST, PUT, DELETE) for **RESTful APIs**.

Example: Handling GET and POST Requests

go
CopyEdit
```go
package main

import (
    "fmt"
    "net/http"
)

// GET request handler
func getHandler(w http.ResponseWriter, r *http.Request) {
```

```go
    if r.Method == "GET" {
        fmt.Fprintln(w, "Received a GET request!")
    } else {
        http.Error(w, "Method Not Allowed", http.StatusMethodNotAllowed)
    }
}

// POST request handler
func postHandler(w http.ResponseWriter, r *http.Request) {
    if r.Method == "POST" {
        fmt.Fprintln(w, "Received a POST request!")
    } else {
        http.Error(w, "Method Not Allowed", http.StatusMethodNotAllowed)
    }
}

func main() {
    http.HandleFunc("/get", getHandler)
    http.HandleFunc("/post", postHandler)

    fmt.Println("Server running on port 8080")
    http.ListenAndServe(":8080", nil)
}
```

✔ **Handles GET and POST separately.**
✔ **Returns 405 Method Not Allowed for unsupported methods.**

11.2.3 Reading Query Parameters

Query parameters allow sending **data via the URL**.

Example: Extracting Query Parameters

go
CopyEdit
```go
func queryHandler(w http.ResponseWriter, r *http.Request) {
    name := r.URL.Query().Get("name") // Retrieve query parameter
```

```go
    if name == "" {
        name = "Guest"
    }
    fmt.Fprintf(w, "Hello, %s!", name)
}

func main() {
    http.HandleFunc("/greet", queryHandler)
    http.ListenAndServe(":8080", nil)
}
```

- ◆ **Access via:** http://localhost:8080/greet?name=Alice
- ◆ **Output:** Hello, Alice!

✔ **r.URL.Query().Get("name") extracts query parameters.**
✔ **Returns Guest if no name is provided.**

11.2.4 Handling JSON Requests and Responses

Go's standard library includes encoding/json for handling **JSON APIs**.

Example: Sending JSON Response
go
CopyEdit
```go
package main

import (
    "encoding/json"
    "net/http"
)

type Response struct {
    Message string `json:"message"`
}

func jsonHandler(w http.ResponseWriter, r *http.Request) {
```

```go
    w.Header().Set("Content-Type", "application/json")
    response := Response{Message: "Hello, JSON!"}
    json.NewEncoder(w).Encode(response)
}

func main() {
    http.HandleFunc("/json", jsonHandler)
    http.ListenAndServe(":8080", nil)
}
```

* **Access via:** http://localhost:8080/json
* **Output:** {"message":"Hello, JSON!"}

✔ Sets Content-Type: application/json header.
✔ Encodes struct data into JSON.

11.2.5 Handling Form Data (POST Requests)

Go can **parse form data** sent via application/x-www-form-urlencoded.

Example: Processing Form Data

go
CopyEdit
```go
func formHandler(w http.ResponseWriter, r *http.Request) {
    if r.Method != "POST" {
        http.Error(w, "Only POST allowed", http.StatusMethodNotAllowed)
        return
    }

    r.ParseForm()  // Parse form data
    name := r.FormValue("name")
    email := r.FormValue("email")

    response := fmt.Sprintf("Received: Name=%s, Email=%s", name, email)
    fmt.Fprintln(w, response)
}
```

```go
func main() {
    http.HandleFunc("/submit", formHandler)
    http.ListenAndServe(":8080", nil)
}
```

- **Send a POST request with** name=John&email=john@example.com.
- **Returns:** Received: Name=John, Email=john@example.com

✔ r.ParseForm() **extracts form values.**
✔ r.FormValue("name") **retrieves specific fields.**

11.2.6 Gracefully Shutting Down the Server

By default, http.ListenAndServe() runs **indefinitely**. To **gracefully shut down** on system signals (e.g., CTRL+C), use http.Server.

Example: Graceful Shutdown

go
CopyEdit
```go
package main

import (
    "context"
    "fmt"
    "net/http"
    "os"
    "os/signal"
    "time"
)

func main() {
    server := &http.Server{Addr: ":8080"}

    go func() {
        fmt.Println("Server running on port 8080")
```

```
    if err := server.ListenAndServe(); err != http.ErrServerClosed {
        fmt.Println("Server error:", err)
    }
}()

stop := make(chan os.Signal, 1)
signal.Notify(stop, os.Interrupt)
<-stop

fmt.Println("Shutting down server...")
ctx, cancel := context.WithTimeout(context.Background(), 5*time.Second)
defer cancel()
server.Shutdown(ctx)
}
```

✔ **Ensures cleanup before shutdown.**
✔ **Uses signal.Notify() to detect CTRL+C.**

✔ **Go provides a built-in web server using net/http.**
✔ **Supports handling routes, JSON, query parameters, and form data.**
✔ **Graceful shutdown prevents abrupt terminations**

11.3 Handling HTTP Requests and Responses

The core of any web application is handling HTTP requests and returning appropriate responses. Go's net/http package provides a simple way to manage different HTTP methods (GET, POST, PUT, DELETE) and work with headers, body, and query parameters.

11.3.1 Understanding HTTP Requests in Go

Each HTTP request contains the following key components:

Request Component	Description
Method	Specifies the type of request (GET , POST , PUT , etc.).
Headers	Metadata such as Content-Type and Authorization .
Body	Contains form data, JSON payloads, or other information.
Query Parameters	Key-value pairs passed via the URL.
Path Parameters	Dynamic parts of the URL (e.g., /user/{id}).

11.3.2 Reading Request Headers

The r.Header object provides access to request headers.

Example: Retrieving Request Headers

go

CopyEdit

```go
func headerHandler(w http.ResponseWriter, r *http.Request) {

    userAgent := r.Header.Get("User-Agent")

    fmt.Fprintf(w, "User-Agent: %s", userAgent)

}


func main() {

    http.HandleFunc("/headers", headerHandler)

    http.ListenAndServe(":8080", nil)

}
```

✔ Retrieves the User-Agent header from the request.
✔ Returns it in the HTTP response.

11.3.3 Parsing Query Parameters

Query parameters allow clients to send additional data via the URL.

Example: Handling Query Parameters

go

CopyEdit

```go
func queryHandler(w http.ResponseWriter, r *http.Request) {
    name := r.URL.Query().Get("name")
    if name == "" {
        name = "Guest"
    }
    fmt.Fprintf(w, "Hello, %s!", name)
}

func main() {
    http.HandleFunc("/greet", queryHandler)
    http.ListenAndServe(":8080", nil)
}
```

✔ **Access via:** http://localhost:8080/greet?name=Alice
✔ **Returns:** "Hello, Alice!"

11.3.4 Handling JSON Requests

For REST APIs, requests often include JSON payloads in the body.

Example: Parsing JSON Requests

go

CopyEdit

```go
import (
    "encoding/json"

    "fmt"

    "net/http"
)


type User struct {
    Name  string `json:"name"`

    Email string `json:"email"`
}


func jsonHandler(w http.ResponseWriter, r *http.Request) {
```

```go
if r.Method != "POST" {
    http.Error(w, "Invalid request method", http.StatusMethodNotAllowed)
    return
}

var user User
err := json.NewDecoder(r.Body).Decode(&user)
if err != nil {
    http.Error(w, "Error decoding JSON", http.StatusBadRequest)
    return
}

fmt.Fprintf(w, "Received: Name=%s, Email=%s", user.Name, user.Email)
}

func main() {
    http.HandleFunc("/json", jsonHandler)
    http.ListenAndServe(":8080", nil)
}
```

✔ **Reads JSON from request body using** json.NewDecoder().
✔ **Returns extracted values in the response.**

11.3.5 Sending Custom HTTP Responses

Go allows setting status codes, headers, and response bodies.

Example: Setting Custom Responses

go

CopyEdit

```go
func responseHandler(w http.ResponseWriter, r *http.Request) {
    w.Header().Set("Content-Type", "application/json")
    w.WriteHeader(http.StatusOK)

    response := map[string]string{"message": "Success"}
    json.NewEncoder(w).Encode(response)
}

func main() {
    http.HandleFunc("/response", responseHandler)
    http.ListenAndServe(":8080", nil)
}
```

✔ Sets Content-Type: application/json.
✔ Returns HTTP 200 OK with a JSON response.

11.4 Working with APIs and JSON Parsing

Modern web applications heavily use RESTful APIs for communication between frontend and backend services.

11.4.1 Consuming External APIs

Go's net/http package allows calling external APIs.

Example: Fetching Data from an API

go

CopyEdit

```
import (

    "encoding/json"

    "fmt"

    "net/http"

)


type Joke struct {

    ID   string `json:"id"`

    Joke string `json:"joke"`

}


func fetchJoke() {

    resp, err := http.Get("https://icanhazdadjoke.com/")
```

```go
    if err != nil {
        fmt.Println("Error fetching API:", err)
        return
    }
    defer resp.Body.Close()

    var joke Joke
    json.NewDecoder(resp.Body).Decode(&joke)

    fmt.Println("Joke:", joke.Joke)
}

func main() {
    fetchJoke()
}
```

✔ **Calls** https://icanhazdadjoke.com/ **API and decodes the response into a struct.**

11.4.2 Making a POST Request to an API

go

CopyEdit

```go
import (
```

```go
    "bytes"

    "encoding/json"

    "fmt"

    "net/http"

)


type RequestBody struct {

    Name string `json:"name"`

}


func sendPostRequest() {

    data := RequestBody{Name: "Alice"}

    jsonData, _ := json.Marshal(data)


    resp, err := http.Post("https://api.example.com/submit", "application/json", bytes.NewBuffer(jsonData))

    if err != nil {

        fmt.Println("Error:", err)

        return

    }

    defer resp.Body.Close()
```

```go
    fmt.Println("Response status:", resp.Status)

}


func main() {

    sendPostRequest()

}
```

✔ **Encodes Go struct into JSON and sends a POST request.**

11.5 Adding Middleware for Authentication and Logging

Middleware functions wrap HTTP handlers to add additional behavior like logging, authentication, or request modification.

11.5.1 What is Middleware?

Middleware is a function that intercepts HTTP requests before they reach the final handler.

Use Case	Description
Logging	Tracks incoming requests.
Authentication	Verifies user credentials.
CORS Handling	Allows cross-origin requests.

11.5.2 Creating Logging Middleware

Example: Request Logging Middleware

go

CopyEdit

```go
func loggingMiddleware(next http.Handler) http.Handler {
    return http.HandlerFunc(func(w http.ResponseWriter, r *http.Request) {
        fmt.Printf("Request: %s %s\n", r.Method, r.URL.Path)
        next.ServeHTTP(w, r)  // Call next handler
    })
}


func helloHandler(w http.ResponseWriter, r *http.Request) {
    fmt.Fprintln(w, "Hello, World!")
}


func main() {
    mux := http.NewServeMux()
    mux.HandleFunc("/", helloHandler)

    wrappedMux := loggingMiddleware(mux)  // Apply middleware
    http.ListenAndServe(":8080", wrappedMux)
}
```

✔ Logs all incoming requests.
✔ Middleware is applied before serving requests.

11.5.3 Implementing Authentication Middleware

Example: Simple Authentication Middleware

go

CopyEdit

```go
func authMiddleware(next http.Handler) http.Handler {
    return http.HandlerFunc(func(w http.ResponseWriter, r *http.Request) {
        token := r.Header.Get("Authorization")
        if token != "Bearer secret123" {
            http.Error(w, "Unauthorized", http.StatusUnauthorized)
            return
        }
        next.ServeHTTP(w, r)
    })
}


func secretHandler(w http.ResponseWriter, r *http.Request) {
    fmt.Fprintln(w, "Welcome to the secret page!")
}
```

```
func main() {

    mux := http.NewServeMux()

    mux.HandleFunc("/secret", secretHandler)


    http.ListenAndServe(":8080", authMiddleware(mux))

}
```

✔ Blocks access unless a valid Authorization header is provided.

✔ Go provides a powerful net/http package for handling requests and responses.
✔ APIs can be easily consumed using http.Get and http.Post.
✔ Middleware helps add logging, authentication, and security

Chapter 12: Building CLI Applications in Go

Go is an excellent choice for building **command-line interface (CLI) applications** due to its simplicity, efficiency, and built-in support for handling system-level operations. CLI applications are widely used for automation, DevOps tasks, system administration, and development workflows.

This chapter covers the fundamentals of **CLI development**, including **parsing command-line arguments**, handling **user input**, and structuring CLI applications efficiently.

12.1 Introduction to Command-Line Interfaces

A **command-line interface (CLI) application** is a program that runs in a **terminal or shell** and takes user input in the form of **commands and flags**.

12.1.1 Why Build CLI Applications in Go?

■ **Fast Execution** – Go is compiled, making CLI tools very fast.
■ **Static Binaries** – Go produces standalone executables without external dependencies.
■ **Cross-Platform** – CLI applications can run on Windows, macOS, and Linux.
■ **Built-in Support** – Go's flag and os packages handle command-line input natively.

12.1.2 Basic Structure of a CLI Application

Every CLI application in Go typically follows this structure:

1. **Read input (arguments, flags, or user input)**
2. **Process the input**
3. **Output a result or perform an action**

Example: A Simple CLI Program

go
CopyEdit
```
package main

import (
    "fmt"
    "os"
)

func main() {
    fmt.Println("Hello, CLI!")  // Print message to terminal
    fmt.Println("Arguments:", os.Args)  // Print all command-line arguments
}
```

✔ Run it with:

sh
CopyEdit
```
go run main.go
```

✔ Pass arguments:

sh
CopyEdit
```
go run main.go arg1 arg2
```

✔ Output:

go
CopyEdit
```
Hello, CLI!
Arguments: [main.go arg1 arg2]
```

🚀 **os.Args provides access to command-line arguments.**

12.2 Parsing Arguments and User Input

CLI applications often need to **accept arguments** and **parse user input**. Go provides two built-in ways to do this:

1. os.Args – Accesses raw command-line arguments.
2. flag **package** – Parses command-line flags easily.

12.2.1 Using os.Args to Read Arguments

The os.Args slice contains **all command-line arguments**, where:

- os.Args[0] is the program's name.
- os.Args[1] onwards are the user-provided arguments.

Example: Printing Command-Line Arguments
go
CopyEdit

```go
package main

import (
    "fmt"
    "os"
)

func main() {
    args := os.Args  // Get command-line arguments
    fmt.Println("Program Name:", args[0])

    if len(args) > 1 {
        fmt.Println("Arguments:", args[1:])
    } else {
        fmt.Println("No arguments provided.")
    }
}
```

✔ Run it with arguments:

sh
CopyEdit
```
go run main.go hello world
```

✔ Output:

less
CopyEdit
```
Program Name: main.go
Arguments: [hello world]
```

🔔 **Issue:** Raw arguments require manual parsing.

12.2.2 Using flag for Parsing Command-Line Flags

Go's flag package provides an easy way to define and parse **flags** (e.g., -name, -count, -debug).

Example: Parsing Flags

go
CopyEdit
```go
package main

import (
    "flag"
    "fmt"
)

func main() {
    name := flag.String("name", "Guest", "Your name")
    age := flag.Int("age", 30, "Your age")
    debug := flag.Bool("debug", false, "Enable debug mode")

    flag.Parse() // Parse command-line flags
```

```go
    fmt.Println("Name:", *name)
    fmt.Println("Age:", *age)
    fmt.Println("Debug Mode:", *debug)
}
```

✔ Run it with flags:

sh
CopyEdit
```
go run main.go -name=Alice -age=25 -debug
```

✔ Output:

yaml
CopyEdit
```
Name: Alice
Age: 25
Debug Mode: true
```

🚀 **Best Practice:** Always call flag.Parse() before using flag values.

12.2.3 Handling Positional Arguments with flag.Args()

flag.Args() returns **non-flag arguments** (extra arguments after flags).

Example: Using Positional Arguments

go
CopyEdit
```go
func main() {
    flag.Parse()
    args := flag.Args()

    if len(args) == 0 {
        fmt.Println("No extra arguments provided.")
```

```
        return
    }

    fmt.Println("Extra arguments:", args)
}
```

✔ Run it with extra arguments:

sh
CopyEdit
```
go run main.go -name=Bob extra1 extra2
```

✔ Output:

less
CopyEdit
```
Extra arguments: [extra1 extra2]
```

12.2.4 Handling User Input with bufio.Scanner

Some CLI tools require **interactive user input**. Go's bufio.Scanner makes reading user input easy.

Example: Reading Input from the User

go
CopyEdit
```
package main

import (
    "bufio"
    "fmt"
    "os"
)

func main() {
```

```go
reader := bufio.NewScanner(os.Stdin)

fmt.Print("Enter your name: ")
reader.Scan() // Read user input
name := reader.Text()

fmt.Println("Hello,", name)
}
```

✔ Run it:

sh
CopyEdit
```sh
go run main.go
```

✔ Input:

yaml
CopyEdit
```
Enter your name: Alice
```

✔ Output:

CopyEdit
```
Hello, Alice
```

🚀 **Best Practice:** Always check for errors when using Scan():

go
CopyEdit
```go
if err := reader.Err(); err != nil {
    fmt.Println("Error reading input:", err)
}
```

12.2.5 Checking for Required Arguments

To enforce **mandatory arguments,** check the length of os.Args or flag.Args().

Example: Enforcing Required Arguments

go
CopyEdit

```go
package main

import (
    "fmt"
    "os"
)

func main() {
    if len(os.Args) < 2 {
        fmt.Println("Usage: go run main.go <your name>")
        os.Exit(1)  // Exit with error code
    }

    fmt.Println("Hello,", os.Args[1])
}
```

✔ Run without arguments:

sh
CopyEdit

```sh
go run main.go
```

✔ Output:

go
CopyEdit

```
Usage: go run main.go <your name>
```

🖋 **Best Practice:** Use os.Exit(1) for errors.

✔ Go makes CLI development easy with os.Args and flag.
✔ Use flag for structured argument parsing.
✔ Use bufio.Scanner for interactive user input.
✔ Always validate and handle errors properly.

12.3 Handling Configuration Files (YAML, JSON)

CLI applications often need to **store settings** or **load configurations** from external files. Go provides built-in support for **JSON**, and third-party libraries like gopkg.in/yaml.v3 help handle **YAML** configurations.

12.3.1 Why Use Configuration Files?

* **Persistent Settings** – Avoids hardcoding values.
* **Environment-Specific Configurations** – Different settings for development, testing, and production.
* **Easier Customization** – Users can modify configs without recompiling.

12.3.2 Reading Configuration from a JSON File

Go's encoding/json package allows easy **parsing of JSON configuration files**.

Example: Loading JSON Configuration

config.json

```json
CopyEdit
{
  "app_name": "MyCLIApp",
  "port": 8080,
  "debug": true
}
```

Go Code to Load JSON:

```go
go
CopyEdit
package main

import (
    "encoding/json"
    "fmt"
    "os"
)

type Config struct {
    AppName string `json:"app_name"`
    Port    int    `json:"port"`
    Debug   bool   `json:"debug"`
}

func loadConfig(filename string) (*Config, error) {
    file, err := os.Open(filename)
    if err != nil {
        return nil, err
    }
    defer file.Close()

    var config Config
    decoder := json.NewDecoder(file)
    err = decoder.Decode(&config)
    if err != nil {
        return nil, err
    }

    return &config, nil
}

func main() {
    config, err := loadConfig("config.json")
    if err != nil {
```

```go
        fmt.Println("Error loading config:", err)
        os.Exit(1)
    }

    fmt.Println("App Name:", config.AppName)
    fmt.Println("Port:", config.Port)
    fmt.Println("Debug Mode:", config.Debug)
}
```

✔ **Reads JSON from config.json and maps it to a struct.**
✔ **json.NewDecoder() efficiently parses JSON files.**
✔ **Gracefully handles file errors.**

12.3.3 Reading Configuration from a YAML File

YAML is commonly used for configurations due to its **readability and simplicity**. The gopkg.in/yaml.v3 package provides YAML parsing support.

Example: Loading YAML Configuration

config.yaml

```yaml
yaml
CopyEdit
app_name: MyCLIApp
port: 8080
debug: true
```

Go Code to Load YAML:

```go
go
CopyEdit
package main

import (
    "fmt"
```

```go
    "os"

    "gopkg.in/yaml.v3"
)

type Config struct {
    AppName string `yaml:"app_name"`
    Port    int    `yaml:"port"`
    Debug   bool   `yaml:"debug"`
}

func loadYAMLConfig(filename string) (*Config, error) {
    file, err := os.ReadFile(filename)
    if err != nil {
        return nil, err
    }

    var config Config
    err = yaml.Unmarshal(file, &config)
    if err != nil {
        return nil, err
    }

    return &config, nil
}

func main() {
    config, err := loadYAMLConfig("config.yaml")
    if err != nil {
        fmt.Println("Error loading config:", err)
        os.Exit(1)
    }

    fmt.Println("App Name:", config.AppName)
    fmt.Println("Port:", config.Port)
    fmt.Println("Debug Mode:", config.Debug)
}
```

✔ Uses gopkg.in/yaml.v3 **for YAML parsing.**
✔ **Reads configuration values and maps them to a struct.**

12.3.4 Using Environment Variables for Configuration

Some settings should not be stored in config files (e.g., API keys, credentials). Instead, use **environment variables**.

Example: Reading Environment Variables

go
CopyEdit

```go
package main

import (
    "fmt"
    "os"
)

func main() {
    dbHost := os.Getenv("DB_HOST")
    if dbHost == "" {
        dbHost = "localhost"  // Default value if not set
    }

    fmt.Println("Database Host:", dbHost)
}
```

✔ **Retrieves** DB_HOST **from environment variables.**
✔ **Falls back to** "localhost" **if** DB_HOST **is not set.**

12.4 Automating Tasks with CLI Applications

Go's performance and simplicity make it **ideal for task automation**. Many DevOps tools, data-processing scripts, and deployment utilities are built in Go.

12.4.1 Common Use Cases for Automation

■ **File Processing** – Parsing logs, generating reports.
■ **System Administration** – Managing users, services, and system status.
■ **Data Scraping** – Fetching and processing data from APIs or web pages.
■ **Deployment Scripts** – Automating builds, deployments, and backups.

12.4.2 Automating File Processing

Go can **read, modify, and write files** efficiently, making it great for **log processing and report generation**.

Example: Processing a Log File
go
CopyEdit
```
package main

import (
    "bufio"
    "fmt"
    "os"
    "strings"
)

func processLogFile(filename string) {
    file, err := os.Open(filename)
    if err != nil {
        fmt.Println("Error opening file:", err)
        return
    }
    defer file.Close()

    scanner := bufio.NewScanner(file)
    for scanner.Scan() {
        line := scanner.Text()
```

```go
        if strings.Contains(line, "ERROR") {
            fmt.Println("Found error log:", line)
        }
    }

    if err := scanner.Err(); err != nil {
        fmt.Println("Error reading file:", err)
    }
}

func main() {
    processLogFile("server.log")
}
```

✔ **Reads** server.log, **searches for "ERROR" messages.**
✔ **Uses** bufio.Scanner **for efficient line-by-line processing.**

12.4.3 Automating HTTP Requests

Go's net/http package can automate **fetching and processing API responses**.

Example: Fetching Weather Data
go
CopyEdit
```go
package main

import (
    "encoding/json"
    "fmt"
    "net/http"
)

type WeatherResponse struct {
    Temperature float64 `json:"temp"`
    City        string  `json:"city"`
}
```

```go
func fetchWeather() {
    resp, err := http.Get("https://api.weather.com/example")
    if err != nil {
        fmt.Println("Error fetching weather:", err)
        return
    }
    defer resp.Body.Close()

    var weather WeatherResponse
    json.NewDecoder(resp.Body).Decode(&weather)

    fmt.Printf("Weather in %s: %.2f°C\n", weather.City, weather.Temperature)
}

func main() {
    fetchWeather()
}
```

✔ **Fetches weather data from an API and parses JSON response.**
✔ **Automates API interaction without a browser.**

12.4.4 Scheduling Automated Tasks

Go **lacks built-in cron jobs,** but external libraries like robfig/cron allow task scheduling.

Example: Running a Task Every Minute
go
CopyEdit
```go
package main

import (
    "fmt"
    "time"
)
```

```go
func task() {
    fmt.Println("Running scheduled task at", time.Now())
}

func main() {
    ticker := time.NewTicker(1 * time.Minute) // Run every minute
    defer ticker.Stop()

    for range ticker.C {
        task()
    }
}
```

✔ **Runs a task every minute using** time.Ticker.

12.4.5 Creating a CLI Task Runner

A **task runner** can automate multiple tasks using CLI commands.

Example: Simple CLI Task Runner
go
CopyEdit
```go
package main

import (
    "fmt"
    "os"
)

func backupTask() {
    fmt.Println("Running backup task...")
}

func cleanupTask() {
    fmt.Println("Running cleanup task...")
```

```go
}

func main() {
    if len(os.Args) < 2 {
        fmt.Println("Usage: go run main.go <task>")
        os.Exit(1)
    }

    switch os.Args[1] {
    case "backup":
        backupTask()
    case "cleanup":
        cleanupTask()
    default:
        fmt.Println("Unknown task:", os.Args[1])
    }
}
```

✔ **Allows running predefined tasks like** backup **and** cleanup.
✔ **Run with:**

sh
CopyEdit
go run main.go backup

✔ **Go handles JSON, YAML, and environment variables for configurations.**
✔ **CLI tools can automate file processing, API calls, and scheduling.**
✔ **Use Go's** os, flag, **and** net/http **for automation**

Chapter 13: Database Integration with Go

Databases are an essential part of most applications, storing and managing structured data efficiently. Go provides robust support for interacting with relational databases such as **SQLite, PostgreSQL, and MySQL** through the database/sql package and various drivers.

This chapter covers the fundamentals of **database integration in Go**, including setting up database connections, executing queries, and handling transactions.

13.1 Introduction to Databases in Go

13.1.1 Why Use a Database in Go?

Databases allow applications to **store, retrieve, update, and delete** data efficiently. Some common use cases for databases in Go include:

■ **Web Applications** – Storing user accounts, products, or logs.
■ **CLI Tools** – Saving configuration data and task records.
■ **APIs & Microservices** – Managing data persistence across multiple services.
■ **Data Analytics** – Processing structured information.

13.1.2 Go's database/sql **Package**

Go's **standard library** provides the database/sql package, which acts as a common interface for SQL databases. It supports multiple database drivers via **third-party adapters**.

Common Database Drivers for Go

Database	Driver
SQLite	github.com/mattn/go-sqlite3
PostgreSQL	github.com/lib/pq
MySQL	github.com/go-sql-driver/mysql

🚀 **Best Practice:** Always use database/sql with a driver to interact with databases efficiently.

13.1.3 Setting Up a Database Connection

Every database connection in Go follows a similar pattern:

1. **Import the necessary driver**
2. **Initialize a connection**
3. **Handle errors properly**
4. **Close the connection when done**

Example: Connecting to a Database

go
CopyEdit
```go
package main

import (
    "database/sql"
    "fmt"
    "log"

    _ "github.com/lib/pq"  // PostgreSQL driver
)

func main() {
    dsn := "user=postgres password=secret dbname=mydb sslmode=disable"
    db, err := sql.Open("postgres", dsn)
    if err != nil {
        log.Fatal("Error connecting to database:", err)
    }
    defer db.Close()

    fmt.Println("Connected to database successfully!")
}
```

✔ **sql.Open("postgres", dsn)** initializes a PostgreSQL connection.
✔ **Always defer** db.Close() **to clean up resources.**

13.2 Working with SQLite, PostgreSQL, and MySQL

Each database has unique characteristics and is suited for different use cases:

Database	Driver
SQLite	github.com/mattn/go-sqlite3
PostgreSQL	github.com/lib/pq
MySQL	github.com/go-sql-driver/mysql

13.2.1 Working with SQLite in Go

SQLite is a **lightweight, file-based** database. It does not require a separate database server, making it ideal for **small-scale applications**.

Installing SQLite Driver
sh
CopyEdit
go get github.com/mattn/go-sqlite3

Example: Connecting to SQLite
go
CopyEdit

```
package main

import (
    "database/sql"
    "fmt"
    "log"

    _ "github.com/mattn/go-sqlite3"
)

func main() {
    db, err := sql.Open("sqlite3", "test.db")
    if err != nil {
```

```go
        log.Fatal(err)
    }
    defer db.Close()

    fmt.Println("Connected to SQLite database!")
}
```

✔ Creates **test.db** file automatically if it doesn't exist.
✔ Does not require a separate database server.

Creating a Table in SQLite

go
CopyEdit
```go
func createTable(db *sql.DB) {
    query := `
    CREATE TABLE IF NOT EXISTS users (
        id INTEGER PRIMARY KEY AUTOINCREMENT,
        name TEXT,
        email TEXT UNIQUE
    );`
    _, err := db.Exec(query)
    if err != nil {
        log.Fatal("Error creating table:", err)
    }
    fmt.Println("Table created successfully")
}
```

13.2.2 Working with PostgreSQL in Go

PostgreSQL is a **powerful, open-source relational database** known for **performance, scalability, and extensibility**.

Installing PostgreSQL Driver

sh
CopyEdit
```sh
go get github.com/lib/pq
```

Example: Connecting to PostgreSQL

go
CopyEdit
```go
package main

import (
    "database/sql"
    "fmt"
    "log"

    _ "github.com/lib/pq"
)

func main() {
    connStr := "user=postgres password=secret dbname=mydb sslmode=disable"
    db, err := sql.Open("postgres", connStr)
    if err != nil {
        log.Fatal(err)
    }
    defer db.Close()

    fmt.Println("Connected to PostgreSQL!")
}
```

✔ Uses sslmode=disable for local development.

Creating a Table in PostgreSQL

go
CopyEdit
```go
func createTable(db *sql.DB) {
    query := `
```

215

```
CREATE TABLE IF NOT EXISTS users (
    id SERIAL PRIMARY KEY,
    name VARCHAR(50),
    email VARCHAR(100) UNIQUE
);`
_, err := db.Exec(query)
if err != nil {
    log.Fatal("Error creating table:", err)
}
fmt.Println("Table created successfully")
}
```

✔ Uses SERIAL for auto-incrementing primary keys.

13.2.3 Working with MySQL in Go

MySQL is a **widely used relational database** known for **fast read operations and high reliability**.

Installing MySQL Driver
sh
CopyEdit
go get github.com/go-sql-driver/mysql

Example: Connecting to MySQL
go
CopyEdit
```
package main

import (
    "database/sql"
    "fmt"
    "log"

    _ "github.com/go-sql-driver/mysql"
```

```go
)

func main() {
    dsn := "user:password@tcp(localhost:3306)/mydb"
    db, err := sql.Open("mysql", dsn)
    if err != nil {
        log.Fatal(err)
    }
    defer db.Close()

    fmt.Println("Connected to MySQL!")
}
```

✔ Uses **user:password@tcp(host:port)/dbname** as the connection string.

Creating a Table in MySQL

go
CopyEdit
```go
func createTable(db *sql.DB) {
    query := `
    CREATE TABLE IF NOT EXISTS users (
        id INT AUTO_INCREMENT PRIMARY KEY,
        name VARCHAR(50),
        email VARCHAR(100) UNIQUE
    );`
    _, err := db.Exec(query)
    if err != nil {
        log.Fatal("Error creating table:", err)
    }
    fmt.Println("Table created successfully")
}
```

✔ Uses **AUTO_INCREMENT** for primary key generation.

13.2.4 Running Queries in Go

Once connected, we can **insert, retrieve, update, and delete records** in the database.

Inserting Data

go
CopyEdit

```go
func insertUser(db *sql.DB, name, email string) {
    query := "INSERT INTO users (name, email) VALUES ($1, $2)"
    _, err := db.Exec(query, name, email)
    if err != nil {
        log.Fatal("Error inserting user:", err)
    }
    fmt.Println("User added successfully!")
}
```

Fetching Data

go
CopyEdit

```go
func getUsers(db *sql.DB) {
    rows, err := db.Query("SELECT id, name, email FROM users")
    if err != nil {
        log.Fatal(err)
    }
    defer rows.Close()

    for rows.Next() {
        var id int
        var name, email string
        rows.Scan(&id, &name, &email)
        fmt.Printf("ID: %d, Name: %s, Email: %s\n", id, name, email)
    }
}
```

✔ **Go supports SQLite, PostgreSQL, and MySQL using** database/sql.
✔ **Always handle errors when connecting to a database.**
✔ **Use parameterized queries ($1, ?) to prevent SQL injection.**
✔ **Always close connections and rows after execution**

13.3 Connecting to a Database with GORM

GORM is a powerful **ORM (Object-Relational Mapper)** for Go that simplifies database operations by providing an easy-to-use abstraction layer. It supports **automatic migrations, struct-based modeling, and relationships** between tables.

13.3.1 Why Use GORM?

■ **Simplifies SQL queries** – Works with structs instead of raw SQL.
■ **Supports multiple databases** – Compatible with PostgreSQL, MySQL, SQLite, and more.
■ **Automatic table creation** – Handles migrations and schema changes.
■ **Built-in CRUD operations** – Provides methods like Create, Find, Update, and Delete.

13.3.2 Installing GORM and Database Drivers

Before using GORM, install it along with the database driver:

For SQLite
sh
CopyEdit
```
go get -u gorm.io/gorm gorm.io/driver/sqlite
```

For PostgreSQL
sh
CopyEdit
```
go get -u gorm.io/gorm gorm.io/driver/postgres
```

For MySQL

sh
CopyEdit

go get -u gorm.io/gorm gorm.io/driver/mysql

13.3.3 Connecting to a Database with GORM

GORM requires a **DSN (Data Source Name)** to establish a connection.

Example: Connecting to SQLite with GORM

go
CopyEdit

```
package main

import (
    "fmt"
    "gorm.io/driver/sqlite"
    "gorm.io/gorm"
    "log"
)

func main() {
    db, err := gorm.Open(sqlite.Open("test.db"), &gorm.Config{})
    if err != nil {
        log.Fatal("Failed to connect to database:", err)
    }

    fmt.Println("Connected to SQLite database successfully!")
}
```

✔ Uses **gorm.Open(sqlite.Open("test.db"))** **to connect to SQLite.**
✔ **No need to manually** defer db.Close() **as GORM handles connections efficiently.**

Example: Connecting to PostgreSQL with GORM

```go
go
CopyEdit
package main

import (
    "fmt"
    "gorm.io/driver/postgres"
    "gorm.io/gorm"
    "log"
)

func main() {
    dsn := "host=localhost user=postgres password=secret dbname=mydb port=5432 sslmode=disable"
    db, err := gorm.Open(postgres.Open(dsn), &gorm.Config{})
    if err != nil {
        log.Fatal("Failed to connect to PostgreSQL:", err)
    }

    fmt.Println("Connected to PostgreSQL database successfully!")
}
```

✔ Uses **gorm.Open(postgres.Open(dsn))** **for PostgreSQL connections.**
✔ **Provides automatic connection pooling.**

Example: Connecting to MySQL with GORM

```go
go
CopyEdit
package main

import (
    "fmt"
    "gorm.io/driver/mysql"
    "gorm.io/gorm"
    "log"
)
```

```go
func main() {
    dsn :=
"user:password@tcp(127.0.0.1:3306)/mydb?charset=utf8mb4&parseTime=True&loc=L
ocal"
    db, err := gorm.Open(mysql.Open(dsn), &gorm.Config{})
    if err != nil {
        log.Fatal("Failed to connect to MySQL:", err)
    }

    fmt.Println("Connected to MySQL database successfully!")
}
```

✔ Uses **gorm.Open(mysql.Open(dsn))** for MySQL.
✔ Supports additional MySQL options like parseTime=True.

13.4 CRUD Operations in Go

CRUD (**Create, Read, Update, Delete**) operations are the foundation of database applications. GORM provides simple methods for performing these actions.

13.4.1 Defining a Model in GORM

A **GORM model** is a struct that maps to a database table.

Example: User Model
go
CopyEdit
```go
package main

import (
    "gorm.io/gorm"
)

type User struct {
    ID    uint    `gorm:"primaryKey"`
```

```
Name  string `gorm:"size:100"`
Email string `gorm:"unique"`
}
```

✔ **gorm:"primaryKey"** – Marks ID as the primary key.
✔ **gorm:"unique"** – Ensures Email is unique.
✔ **gorm:"size:100"** – Limits the Name field to 100 characters.

13.4.2 Creating Tables with GORM

GORM can **automatically create** tables using **AutoMigrate**.

```go
CopyEdit
func main() {
    db, _ := gorm.Open(sqlite.Open("test.db"), &gorm.Config{})

    db.AutoMigrate(&User{}) // Automatically creates the users table

    fmt.Println("Database migrated successfully!")
}
```

✔ **db.AutoMigrate(&User{})** creates the table if it doesn't exist.
✔ **Works for any database supported by GORM.**

13.4.3 Creating a Record (INSERT)

To insert a new record into the database, use db.Create().

Example: Insert a User

go
CopyEdit
```go
func createUser(db *gorm.DB, name, email string) {
    user := User{Name: name, Email: email}
    db.Create(&user)

    fmt.Println("User added:", user)
}
```

✔ **db.Create(&user)** inserts the record into the users table.

13.4.4 Retrieving Records (SELECT)

GORM provides multiple ways to fetch records from the database.

Example: Retrieve a Single Record

go
CopyEdit
```go
func getUser(db *gorm.DB, id uint) {
    var user User
    result := db.First(&user, id)

    if result.Error != nil {
        fmt.Println("User not found!")
        return
    }

    fmt.Println("User found:", user.Name, user.Email)
}
```

✔ **db.First(&user, id)** retrieves a user by primary key.
✔ **Handles errors if the user does not exist.**

Example: Retrieve Multiple Records

go
CopyEdit
```
func getAllUsers(db *gorm.DB) {
    var users []User
    db.Find(&users)  // Fetch all users

    for _, user := range users {
        fmt.Println(user.ID, user.Name, user.Email)
    }
}
```

✔ db.Find(&users) retrieves all rows from the table.

13.4.5 Updating Records (UPDATE)

To modify existing records, use db.Model().Updates().

Example: Update a User's Email

go
CopyEdit
```
func updateUserEmail(db *gorm.DB, id uint, newEmail string) {
    db.Model(&User{}).Where("id = ?", id).Update("email", newEmail)

    fmt.Println("User email updated successfully!")
}
```

✔ Uses db.Model().Update() to modify a single field.

Example: Update Multiple Fields

go
CopyEdit
```
func updateUser(db *gorm.DB, id uint, name, email string) {
    db.Model(&User{}).Where("id = ?", id).Updates(User{Name: name, Email: email})
```

```go
    fmt.Println("User details updated!")
}
```

✔ Uses Updates() **to modify multiple fields at once.**

13.4.6 Deleting Records (DELETE)

To delete records, use db.Delete().

Example: Delete a User by ID
go
CopyEdit
```go
func deleteUser(db *gorm.DB, id uint) {
    db.Delete(&User{}, id)

    fmt.Println("User deleted!")
}
```

✔ db.Delete(&User{}, id) removes the record permanently.

13.4.7 Running CRUD Operations

Combine all functions in main() to test them.

go
CopyEdit
```go
func main() {
    db, _ := gorm.Open(sqlite.Open("test.db"), &gorm.Config{})
    db.AutoMigrate(&User{})

    createUser(db, "Alice", "alice@example.com")
    getAllUsers(db)
    updateUserEmail(db, 1, "alice@newdomain.com")
    deleteUser(db, 1)
}
```

✔ Executes all CRUD operations sequentially.

✔ GORM simplifies database interactions with ORM capabilities.
✔ Supports multiple databases (SQLite, PostgreSQL, MySQL).
✔ Provides easy-to-use methods for CRUD operations.
✔ Uses AutoMigrate() for automatic schema creation

Chapter 14: Building RESTful APIs in Go

RESTful APIs (Representational State Transfer) allow applications to **communicate over HTTP** in a scalable and efficient way. Go provides powerful tools for building APIs, and the **Gin framework** simplifies the process by offering robust routing, middleware, and request handling.

This chapter covers **REST API development in Go**, including **setting up a basic API using Gin** and implementing essential API features.

14.1 Introduction to REST API Development

14.1.1 What is a REST API?

A **REST API** is a web service that follows **REST principles**, allowing clients (such as web and mobile apps) to perform CRUD operations using **HTTP methods**.

HTTP Method	Action	Usage in REST API
GET	Read data	Fetching records
POST	Create data	Adding new records
PUT	Update data	Modifying existing records
DELETE	Remove data	Deleting records

14.1.2 Why Use Go for REST APIs?

■ **High Performance** – Go is compiled, making it faster than interpreted languages.
■ **Minimal Dependencies** – The net/http package provides built-in HTTP support.
■ **Efficient Concurrency** – Go's goroutines enable handling multiple requests efficiently.
■ **Lightweight Deployment** – Go applications compile into a **single binary**.

14.1.3 REST API Architecture in Go

A well-structured REST API in Go typically consists of:

1. **Routes** – Define URL paths and handlers (e.g., /users, /products).
2. **Handlers** – Functions that process API requests and return responses.
3. **Middleware** – Handles authentication, logging, error handling, etc.
4. **Database Integration** – Uses PostgreSQL, MySQL, or SQLite for data storage.
5. **JSON Encoding & Decoding** – Uses encoding/json for request/response handling.

14.2 Setting Up a Basic API with Gin-Gonic

Gin is a **lightweight web framework** for Go that simplifies API development. It provides **fast routing, middleware support, and JSON handling**.

14.2.1 Installing Gin

To install Gin, run:

```sh
CopyEdit
go get -u github.com/gin-gonic/gin
```

14.2.2 Creating a Basic Gin API

A minimal REST API with Gin:

```go
CopyEdit
package main

import (
    "github.com/gin-gonic/gin"
)
```

```go
func main() {
    r := gin.Default() // Create a new Gin router

    r.GET("/", func(c *gin.Context) {
        c.JSON(200, gin.H{"message": "Welcome to the API"})
    })

    r.Run(":8080") // Start the server on port 8080
}
```

✔ Uses gin.Default() to create a router with logging and recovery middleware.
✔ Handles a GET / request and returns a JSON response.
✔ Runs the server on localhost:8080.

14.2.3 Defining API Endpoints

RESTful APIs use **resource-based routes** for managing data.

Example: Defining Multiple API Routes
go
CopyEdit
```go
func main() {
    r := gin.Default()

    r.GET("/users", getUsers)        // Fetch users
    r.POST("/users", createUser)     // Create user
    r.PUT("/users/:id", updateUser)  // Update user
    r.DELETE("/users/:id", deleteUser) // Delete user

    r.Run(":8080")
}
```

✔ Routes are mapped to specific HTTP methods.
✔ Dynamic parameters (e.g., :id) extract values from URLs.

14.2.4 Handling API Requests & Responses

Fetching All Users (GET /users)

go
CopyEdit

```go
func getUsers(c *gin.Context) {
    users := []gin.H{
        {"id": 1, "name": "Alice"},
        {"id": 2, "name": "Bob"},
    }
    c.JSON(200, users)
}
```

✔ **Returns a JSON response with user data.**

Fetching a Single User by ID (GET /users/:id)

go
CopyEdit

```go
func getUserByID(c *gin.Context) {
    id := c.Param("id") // Extract ID from URL
    user := gin.H{"id": id, "name": "Alice"} // Mock data
    c.JSON(200, user)
}
```

✔ **c.Param("id") extracts id from the request URL.**

Creating a New User (POST /users)

go
CopyEdit

```go
type User struct {
    Name string `json:"name"`
}
```

```go
func createUser(c *gin.Context) {
    var user User
    if err := c.ShouldBindJSON(&user); err != nil {
        c.JSON(400, gin.H{"error": "Invalid input"})
        return
    }

    c.JSON(201, gin.H{"message": "User created", "user": user})
}
```

✔ Uses **c.ShouldBindJSON(&user) to parse JSON request bodies.**
✔ **Validates input before processing.**

Updating an Existing User (PUT /users/:id)

go
CopyEdit
```go
func updateUser(c *gin.Context) {
    id := c.Param("id")
    var user User

    if err := c.ShouldBindJSON(&user); err != nil {
        c.JSON(400, gin.H{"error": "Invalid input"})
        return
    }

    c.JSON(200, gin.H{"message": "User updated", "id": id, "user": user})
}
```

✔ **Extracts id and updates user data.**

Deleting a User (DELETE /users/:id)

go
CopyEdit
```go
func deleteUser(c *gin.Context) {
    id := c.Param("id")
    c.JSON(200, gin.H{"message": "User deleted", "id": id})
}
```

✔ **Handles deleting a record by id.**

14.2.5 Running and Testing the API

1. **Run the API:**

sh
CopyEdit
```sh
go run main.go
```

2. **Test with curl:**

sh
CopyEdit
```sh
curl http://localhost:8080/users
```

✔ **Returns:**

json
CopyEdit
```json
[
    {"id":1, "name":"Alice"},
    {"id":2, "name":"Bob"}
]
```

14.2.6 Adding Middleware for Logging & Security

Middleware enhances API functionality by adding **authentication, logging, and rate-limiting**.

Example: Logging Middleware

go
CopyEdit

```go
func loggingMiddleware(c *gin.Context) {
    fmt.Println("Request:", c.Request.Method, c.Request.URL.Path)
    c.Next() // Proceed to the next middleware or handler
}

func main() {
    r := gin.Default()
    r.Use(loggingMiddleware) // Apply middleware

    r.GET("/users", getUsers)
    r.Run(":8080")
}
```

✔ **Logs all incoming API requests.**

14.2.7 Graceful Shutdown Handling

Use context.WithTimeout to **cleanly shut down the API** on system signals.

Example: Graceful Shutdown

go
CopyEdit

```go
import (
    "context"
    "fmt"
    "github.com/gin-gonic/gin"
    "net/http"
    "os"
```

```
    "os/signal"
    "time"
)

func main() {
    r := gin.Default()
    server := &http.Server{Addr: ":8080", Handler: r}

    go func() {
        if err := server.ListenAndServe(); err != nil && err != http.ErrServerClosed {
            fmt.Println("Server error:", err)
        }
    }()

    quit := make(chan os.Signal, 1)
    signal.Notify(quit, os.Interrupt)
    <-quit
    fmt.Println("Shutting down server...")

    ctx, cancel := context.WithTimeout(context.Background(), 5*time.Second)
    defer cancel()
    server.Shutdown(ctx)
}
```

✔ **Ensures all connections close properly before shutdown.**

✔ **Gin makes REST API development fast and efficient.**
✔ **Supports JSON parsing, middleware, and graceful shutdowns.**
✔ **Handles CRUD operations easily with route handlers.**
✔ **Ensures API security with middleware**

14.3 Implementing CRUD Operations in an API

To build a fully functional REST API, we need to implement **Create, Read, Update, and Delete (CRUD) operations** with a database. We'll use **Gin** for routing and **GORM** for database interaction.

14.3.1 Setting Up the Database

We'll use **GORM** to connect to a database. First, install the required packages:

```sh
CopyEdit
go get -u gorm.io/gorm gorm.io/driver/sqlite
```

14.3.2 Defining the Model

We'll define a **User model** and use GORM to create the corresponding table.

```go
CopyEdit
package main

import (
    "gorm.io/driver/sqlite"
    "gorm.io/gorm"
    "log"
)

var db *gorm.DB

type User struct {
    ID    uint   `gorm:"primaryKey" json:"id"`
    Name  string `json:"name"`
    Email string `gorm:"unique" json:"email"`
}
```

```go
func initDB() {
    var err error
    db, err = gorm.Open(sqlite.Open("users.db"), &gorm.Config{})
    if err != nil {
        log.Fatal("Failed to connect to database:", err)
    }

    db.AutoMigrate(&User{}) // Automatically create the users table
}
```

✔ **Uses SQLite (users.db) for storage.**
✔ **Creates the users table automatically using AutoMigrate().**

14.3.3 Implementing API Handlers

1. Creating a User (POST /users)
go
CopyEdit
```go
import "github.com/gin-gonic/gin"

func createUser(c *gin.Context) {
    var user User
    if err := c.ShouldBindJSON(&user); err != nil {
        c.JSON(400, gin.H{"error": "Invalid request"})
        return
    }

    db.Create(&user)
    c.JSON(201, gin.H{"message": "User created", "user": user})
}
```

✔ **Validates JSON input using ShouldBindJSON().**
✔ **Inserts a new user into the database.**

---

2. Retrieving All Users (GET /users)

go
CopyEdit

```go
func getUsers(c *gin.Context) {
    var users []User
    db.Find(&users)
    c.JSON(200, users)
}
```

✔ **Fetches all users from the database using db.Find(&users).**

3. Retrieving a Single User (GET /users/:id)

go
CopyEdit

```go
func getUserByID(c *gin.Context) {
    id := c.Param("id")
    var user User

    if err := db.First(&user, id).Error; err != nil {
        c.JSON(404, gin.H{"error": "User not found"})
        return
    }

    c.JSON(200, user)
}
```

✔ **Uses db.First(&user, id) to fetch a user by id.**

---

4. Updating a User (PUT /users/:id)

go
CopyEdit

```go
func updateUser(c *gin.Context) {
    id := c.Param("id")
    var user User
```

```go
if err := db.First(&user, id).Error; err != nil {
    c.JSON(404, gin.H{"error": "User not found"})
    return
}

if err := c.ShouldBindJSON(&user); err != nil {
    c.JSON(400, gin.H{"error": "Invalid input"})
    return
}

db.Save(&user)
c.JSON(200, gin.H{"message": "User updated", "user": user})
}
```

✔ Checks if the user exists before updating.
✔ Uses db.Save(&user) to update the record.

---

5. Deleting a User (DELETE /users/:id)

go
CopyEdit

```go
func deleteUser(c *gin.Context) {
    id := c.Param("id")
    var user User

    if err := db.First(&user, id).Error; err != nil {
        c.JSON(404, gin.H{"error": "User not found"})
        return
    }

    db.Delete(&user)
    c.JSON(200, gin.H{"message": "User deleted"})
}
```

✔ Deletes a user using db.Delete(&user).

14.3.4 Registering API Routes

Now, let's set up **Gin routes** to expose these CRUD operations:

go
CopyEdit
```go
func main() {
    initDB()
    r := gin.Default()

    r.POST("/users", createUser)
    r.GET("/users", getUsers)
    r.GET("/users/:id", getUserByID)
    r.PUT("/users/:id", updateUser)
    r.DELETE("/users/:id", deleteUser)

    r.Run(":8080")
}
```

✔ **Runs the API on port 8080.**
✔ **Exposes CRUD endpoints for managing users.**

14.4 Authentication and JWT in Go APIs

APIs often require **authentication** to secure access. We'll use **JWT (JSON Web Tokens)** to authenticate users.

14.4.1 Installing JWT Package

sh
CopyEdit
```sh
go get github.com/golang-jwt/jwt/v5
```

14.4.2 Generating JWT Tokens

JWT Secret Key

go
CopyEdit

```go
var jwtSecret = []byte("mysecretkey")
```

Function to Generate a JWT Token

go
CopyEdit

```go
import "github.com/golang-jwt/jwt/v5"

func generateToken(email string) (string, error) {
    token := jwt.NewWithClaims(jwt.SigningMethodHS256, jwt.MapClaims{
        "email": email,
        "exp":   time.Now().Add(time.Hour * 2).Unix(), // Expires in 2 hours
    })

    return token.SignedString(jwtSecret)
}
```

✔ Uses HS256 to sign tokens.
✔ Includes expiration time (exp).

14.4.3 Creating a Login Endpoint (POST /login)

go
CopyEdit

```go
func login(c *gin.Context) {
    var user User
    if err := c.ShouldBindJSON(&user); err != nil {
        c.JSON(400, gin.H{"error": "Invalid input"})
        return
    }

    var dbUser User
```

241

```go
    if err := db.Where("email = ?", user.Email).First(&dbUser).Error; err != nil {
        c.JSON(401, gin.H{"error": "User not found"})
        return
    }

    token, err := generateToken(user.Email)
    if err != nil {
        c.JSON(500, gin.H{"error": "Failed to generate token"})
        return
    }

    c.JSON(200, gin.H{"token": token})
}
```

✔ **Validates user login and returns a JWT token.**

14.4.4 Protecting Routes with JWT Middleware

go
CopyEdit

```go
func authMiddleware(c *gin.Context) {
    tokenString := c.GetHeader("Authorization")
    if tokenString == "" {
        c.JSON(401, gin.H{"error": "Missing token"})
        c.Abort()
        return
    }

    token, err := jwt.Parse(tokenString, func(token *jwt.Token) (interface{}, error) {
        return jwtSecret, nil
    })

    if err != nil || !token.Valid {
        c.JSON(401, gin.H{"error": "Invalid token"})
        c.Abort()
        return
    }
```

```
  c.Next()
}
```

✔ **Checks if the request contains a valid JWT token.**

14.4.5 Applying Authentication Middleware

go
CopyEdit
```
func main() {
  initDB()
  r := gin.Default()

  r.POST("/login", login)
  authorized := r.Group("/")
  authorized.Use(authMiddleware)
  authorized.GET("/users", getUsers)

  r.Run(":8080")
}
```

✔ **Now, GET /users requires authentication.**

14.5 Testing and Debugging APIs

14.5.1 Testing with curl

sh
CopyEdit
```
curl -X POST http://localhost:8080/users -d
'{"name":"Alice","email":"alice@example.com"}' -H "Content-Type: application/json"
```

✔ **Creates a user via API.**

14.5.2 Debugging with Logging

go
CopyEdit
r.Use(gin.Logger())

✔ **Logs API requests for debugging.**

14.5.3 Using Postman for API Testing

1. **Open Postman.**
2. **Send requests to** http://localhost:8080/users.
3. **Check JSON responses.**

✔ **Implemented full CRUD functionality.**
✔ **Added JWT authentication.**
✔ **Used logging and debugging techniques**

Chapter 15: Testing and Debugging Go Applications

Testing and debugging are crucial aspects of software development, ensuring that applications function as expected and perform efficiently. Go provides built-in support for testing, benchmarking, and debugging, making it easy to maintain robust applications.

This chapter covers **unit testing with the** testing **package, benchmarking for performance analysis**, and **debugging Go applications efficiently**.

15.1 Writing Unit Tests with the testing Package

Unit testing verifies that individual functions work as expected. Go's testing package provides a **lightweight and efficient** way to write and run tests.

15.1.1 Creating a Test File

■ **Test files must end with** _test.go (e.g., math_test.go).
■ **Test functions should start with** Test **and take** *testing.T **as a parameter.**

Example: Function to Test
go
CopyEdit
```
package mathutil

func Add(a, b int) int {
    return a + b
}
```

Writing a Unit Test (mathutil_test.go)

go
CopyEdit
```go
package mathutil

import "testing"

func TestAdd(t *testing.T) {
    result := Add(2, 3)
    expected := 5

    if result != expected {
        t.Errorf("Expected %d, got %d", expected, result)
    }
}
```

✔ **t.Errorf() reports failures.**
✔ **No assertion library needed—Go uses basic conditionals.**

15.1.2 Running Unit Tests

Run all tests in a package:

sh
CopyEdit
```sh
go test ./...
```

Run tests in a specific file:

sh
CopyEdit
```sh
go test -v mathutil_test.go
```

✔ **-v enables verbose output.**

15.1.3 Table-Driven Tests

Go developers often use **table-driven tests** to check multiple cases efficiently.

go
CopyEdit
```go
func TestAddCases(t *testing.T) {
    cases := []struct {
        a, b, expected int
    }{
        {2, 3, 5},
        {-1, 1, 0},
        {10, 20, 30},
    }

    for _, c := range cases {
        result := Add(c.a, c.b)
        if result != c.expected {
            t.Errorf("Add(%d, %d) = %d; want %d", c.a, c.b, result, c.expected)
        }
    }
}
```

✔ **Loops through test cases automatically.**
✔ **Improves readability and reduces redundancy.**

15.1.4 Testing HTTP Handlers

For API testing, use httptest.

Example: Testing a Gin Handler
go
CopyEdit
```go
package main

import (
```

```
    "net/http"
    "net/http/httptest"
    "testing"

    "github.com/gin-gonic/gin"
    "github.com/stretchr/testify/assert"
)

func TestHelloHandler(t *testing.T) {
    router := gin.Default()
    router.GET("/hello", helloHandler)

    req, _ := http.NewRequest("GET", "/hello", nil)
    w := httptest.NewRecorder()
    router.ServeHTTP(w, req)

    assert.Equal(t, 200, w.Code)
    assert.JSONEq(t, `{"message": "Hello, World!"}`, w.Body.String())
}
```

✔ Uses httptest.NewRecorder() to simulate API requests.
✔ assert.JSONEq() ensures JSON output matches expected response.

15.2 Benchmarking and Profiling Performance

Benchmarking helps measure function execution speed, while profiling identifies
performance bottlenecks.

15.2.1 Writing Benchmark Tests

Benchmarks follow this pattern:

go
CopyEdit

```
func BenchmarkFunctionName(b *testing.B) { ... }
```

Example: Benchmarking a Function

go
CopyEdit

```
func BenchmarkAdd(b *testing.B) {
  for i := 0; i < b.N; i++ {
    Add(100, 200)
  }
}
```

✔ **b.N runs the function multiple times to gather performance data.**

15.2.2 Running Benchmarks

Run benchmarks using:

sh
CopyEdit

```
go test -bench .
```

Example output:

bash
CopyEdit

```
BenchmarkAdd-8   20000000   100 ns/op
```

✔ **Shows how many iterations ran (20000000) and time per operation (100 ns).**

15.2.3 Profiling with pprof

The pprof package helps analyze CPU and memory usage.

Enable Profiling in a Go Program

go
CopyEdit

```
import (
  "log"
  "net/http"
  _ "net/http/pprof"
)

func main() {
  go func() {
    log.Println(http.ListenAndServe("localhost:6060", nil))
  }()
}
```

✔ **Starts a profiling server on localhost:6060.**

15.2.4 Running Profiling Analysis

Run the CPU profiler:

sh
CopyEdit

```
go tool pprof http://localhost:6060/debug/pprof/profile
```

Run memory profiling:

sh
CopyEdit

```
go tool pprof http://localhost:6060/debug/pprof/heap
```

✔ Generates a performance report for optimization.

15.3 Debugging Go Applications

Debugging helps locate and fix **runtime errors, crashes, and logic bugs**.

15.3.1 Using fmt.Println for Debugging

The simplest method:

```go
CopyEdit
func divide(a, b int) int {
    fmt.Println("Inputs:", a, b)
    return a / b
}
```

✔ Useful for quick debugging but not scalable.

15.3.2 Using log for Better Debugging

The log package adds timestamps and severity levels.

```go
CopyEdit
import "log"

func divide(a, b int) int {
    if b == 0 {
        log.Fatal("Error: Division by zero")
    }
    return a / b
}
```

✔ log.Fatal() **stops execution if an error occurs.**

15.3.3 Using panic and recover for Error Handling

Panic **stops execution** when an error occurs, while recover prevents crashes.

go
CopyEdit
```go
func safeDivide(a, b int) {
    defer func() {
        if err := recover(); err != nil {
            fmt.Println("Recovered from panic:", err)
        }
    }()

    fmt.Println("Result:", a/b)
}
```

✔ **Recovers from runtime errors instead of crashing.**

15.3.4 Using dlv (Delve) for Advanced Debugging

Delve is Go's debugger for stepping through code.

Install Delve

sh
CopyEdit
```sh
go install github.com/go-delve/delve/cmd/dlv@latest
```

Run a Go Program in Debug Mode

sh

CopyEdit

```
dlv debug
```

Set Breakpoints and Step Through Code

sh

CopyEdit

```
b main.go:10  # Set a breakpoint at line 10
c          # Continue execution
n          # Step to the next line
p variable  # Print variable value
```

✔ Helps track variable states and execution flow.

✔ Go's testing package makes unit testing simple.
✔ Benchmarking with go test -bench . helps optimize performance.
✔ Profiling with pprof detects bottlenecks.
✔ Debugging tools like fmt.Println, log, panic/recover, and dlv improve
troubleshootin

Chapter 16: Performance Optimization in Go

Optimizing performance in Go applications involves writing **efficient code, reducing memory usage, and leveraging concurrency effectively**. Go's **garbage collector, memory management, and concurrency model** help build high-performance applications, but developers need to follow best practices to avoid performance bottlenecks.

This chapter covers **writing efficient Go code, optimizing memory usage**, and techniques to improve performance in Go applications.

16.1 Writing Efficient Go Code

Efficient Go code is **fast, memory-efficient, and scalable**. It follows best practices in **algorithm design, data structures, and concurrency management**.

16.1.1 Using Efficient Data Structures

Choosing the right data structure improves both **performance and memory usage**.

Scenario	Efficient Data Structure
Fast lookups	`map[string]int` (hash map)
Sequential storage	`slice` (dynamic array)
Constant time element access	`array`
First-In-First-Out (FIFO)	`list` (linked list)

Example: Using Maps for Fast Lookups

go
CopyEdit
```
func main() {
    users := map[string]int{"Alice": 25, "Bob": 30}
    age := users["Alice"] // O(1) lookup time
```

```
fmt.Println("Alice's Age:", age)
}
```

✔ **Maps provide fast key-based lookups compared to iterating over slices.**

16.1.2 Reducing Unnecessary Allocations

Frequent memory allocations slow down performance and increase **garbage collection overhead**.

Example: Avoiding Unnecessary Allocations

🪣 **Inefficient Code (Allocates Memory on Each Iteration)**

go
CopyEdit
```
for i := 0; i < 1000; i++ {
    s := fmt.Sprintf("Value: %d", i) // Creates a new string each time
    fmt.Println(s)
}
```

⬛ **Optimized Code (Reuses Memory)**

go
CopyEdit
```
s := make([]string, 1000)
for i := 0; i < 1000; i++ {
    s[i] = fmt.Sprintf("Value: %d", i) // Allocates once
}
fmt.Println(s)
```

✔ **Reuses memory instead of repeated allocation.**

16.1.3 Preallocating Memory for Slices

Slices grow dynamically, but frequent **resizing and copying** reduce efficiency.

Example: Preallocating Slice Capacity

go
CopyEdit
```go
nums := make([]int, 0, 1000) // Preallocates space for 1000 elements
for i := 0; i < 1000; i++ {
    nums = append(nums, i)
}
```

✔ **Preallocating avoids repeated reallocation and copying.**

16.1.4 Avoiding Unnecessary Goroutines

Goroutines are lightweight, but creating **too many** can degrade performance.

🔔 **Inefficient Code (Excessive Goroutines)**

go
CopyEdit
```go
for i := 0; i < 100000; i++ {
    go func() {
        fmt.Println("Goroutine:", i) // Unsafe access to `i`
    }()
}
```

⬛ **Optimized Code (Limits Goroutines with a Worker Pool)**

go
CopyEdit
```go
var wg sync.WaitGroup
workerCount := 10
```

256

```
tasks := make(chan int, 100)

for i := 0; i < workerCount; i++ {
    wg.Add(1)
    go func() {
        defer wg.Done()
        for task := range tasks {
            fmt.Println("Processing:", task)
        }
    }()
}

for i := 0; i < 100; i++ {
    tasks <- i
}
close(tasks)
wg.Wait()
```

✔ Uses a worker pool to efficiently process tasks.

16.1.5 Using Efficient String Operations

Strings are immutable, so concatenating large strings can be **slow and memory-intensive**.

🔺 Inefficient Code (String Concatenation in Loops)

go
CopyEdit
```
result := ""
for i := 0; i < 1000; i++ {
    result += fmt.Sprintf("%d", i) // Creates a new string every time
}
```

■ Optimized Code (Using strings.Builder)

go
CopyEdit
```go
var sb strings.Builder
for i := 0; i < 1000; i++ {
    sb.WriteString(fmt.Sprintf("%d", i))
}
result := sb.String()
```

✔ Uses strings.Builder **to build strings efficiently.**

16.1.6 Using Pointers to Avoid Copying Large Data

Passing **large structs** by value causes unnecessary copying.

▲ Inefficient Code (Passes Struct by Value)

go
CopyEdit
```go
type User struct {
    Name  string
    Email string
    Age   int
}

func updateUser(u User) { // Passes by value (copy)
    u.Age = 30
}
```

■ Optimized Code (Passes Struct by Reference)

go
CopyEdit
```go
func updateUser(u *User) { // Passes by reference
    u.Age = 30
}
```

✔ Passing by reference (*User) avoids copying large structs.

16.2 Optimizing Memory Usage

Memory optimization is **critical** for building efficient Go applications, reducing **garbage collection pauses** and improving performance.

16.2.1 Minimizing Garbage Collection Overhead

Go's **garbage collector (GC)** automatically reclaims memory, but frequent allocations increase **GC pressure**.

■ **Best Practices to Reduce GC Overhead**
✔ **Minimize Heap Allocations** – Prefer **value types (struct) over pointers** when possible.
✔ **Use Object Pooling** – Reuse allocated objects instead of repeatedly creating new ones.
✔ **Optimize Slice Capacity** – Preallocate slice capacity to avoid unnecessary reallocation.

16.2.2 Object Pooling with sync.Pool

Using sync.Pool prevents frequent memory allocations by **reusing objects**.

Example: Using sync.Pool
```go
CopyEdit
import (
    "fmt"
    "sync"
)

var userPool = sync.Pool{
    New: func() interface{} {
```

```go
        return &User{}
    },
}

func main() {
    u1 := userPool.Get().(*User) // Retrieve an object from the pool
    u1.Name = "Alice"

    fmt.Println("User:", u1.Name)

    userPool.Put(u1) // Return object to the pool
}
```

✔ **Reduces heap allocations by reusing objects.**

16.2.3 Managing Memory with Slices and Maps

Slices and maps **dynamically allocate memory**, but improper usage leads to **wasted space**.

Freeing Unused Slice Capacity
go
CopyEdit
```go
func shrinkSlice(s []int) []int {
    return append([]int{}, s...) // Creates a new slice with minimal capacity
}
```

✔ **Reduces memory waste by creating a smaller copy.**

Deleting Map Entries to Free Memory
go
CopyEdit
```go
users := map[string]string{"Alice": "Engineer", "Bob": "Doctor"}
delete(users, "Bob") // Frees memory occupied by "Bob"
```

✔ **Removing unused map entries helps free memory.**

16.2.4 Avoiding Memory Leaks

Go **automatically** manages memory, but incorrect usage can still cause memory leaks.

Common Memory Leak Causes

🔺 **Retaining Unused Pointers** – Holding references to objects no longer needed.
🔺 **Infinite Goroutines** – Goroutines that never exit, keeping memory occupied.

Example: Preventing Goroutine Leaks
go
CopyEdit

```go
func startWorker(stop chan bool) {
    for {
        select {
        case <-stop:
            fmt.Println("Stopping worker")
            return
        default:
            // Worker logic here...
        }
    }
}

func main() {
    stop := make(chan bool)
    go startWorker(stop)

    stop <- true // Signal worker to stop
}
```

✔ Using stop <- true **ensures goroutine exits properly.**

✔ **Use efficient data structures (map, slice, sync.Pool) to optimize performance.**
✔ **Preallocate memory to avoid unnecessary allocations.**

✔ Reduce garbage collection pressure by minimizing heap allocations.
✔ Avoid excessive goroutines and memory leaks with proper resource management.

16.3 Profiling CPU and Memory Usage

Profiling helps analyze CPU usage, memory allocation, and performance bottlenecks in Go applications. The pprof package provides built-in profiling tools to collect and analyze runtime statistics.

16.3.1 Enabling CPU and Memory Profiling

Go provides net/http/pprof, which exposes profiling endpoints to analyze CPU, memory, and goroutine usage.

Example: Adding Profiling to a Go Application

go

CopyEdit

```
import (

    "log"

    "net/http"

    _ "net/http/pprof"

)


func main() {

    go func() {
```

```
    log.Println(http.ListenAndServe("localhost:6060", nil)) // Start profiling
server

    }()

    // Your application logic here

    select {} // Keeps the program running

}
```

✔ **Starts a profiling server at** localhost:6060/debug/pprof/.

16.3.2 Collecting CPU Profile Data

To profile CPU usage, run:

sh

CopyEdit

go tool pprof http://localhost:6060/debug/pprof/profile

✔ **Captures a 30-second CPU profile.**

Interactive Pprof Commands

Once inside pprof:

sh

CopyEdit

```
top          # Show top functions consuming CPU

list FuncName  # Show source code of function

web          # Visualize CPU usage graph
```

✔ Identifies which functions consume the most CPU.

16.3.3 Collecting Memory Profile Data

To profile memory allocation, run:

sh

CopyEdit

```
go tool pprof http://localhost:6060/debug/pprof/heap
```

✔ Analyzes heap memory usage.

Find Memory-Hungry Functions

sh

CopyEdit

```
top

list funcName
```

✔ Detects memory-intensive operations and optimizes allocations.

16.3.4 Visualizing Profiles with pprof Web UI

For a graphical analysis, install Graphviz:

sh

CopyEdit

go tool pprof -http=":8081" http://localhost:6060/debug/pprof/profile

✔ Opens an interactive visualization of CPU and memory usage.

16.4 Handling Large Data Processing

Processing large datasets efficiently in Go requires optimized memory management, concurrency, and streaming techniques.

16.4.1 Using Streaming for Large Data Processing

Instead of loading entire datasets into memory, process data in chunks (streaming).

Example: Processing Large Files Line by Line

go

CopyEdit

import (

    "bufio"

```go
	"fmt"
	"os"
)

func processLargeFile(filename string) {
	file, err := os.Open(filename)
	if err != nil {
		fmt.Println("Error:", err)
		return
	}
	defer file.Close()

	scanner := bufio.NewScanner(file)
	for scanner.Scan() {
		processLine(scanner.Text()) // Process each line
	}

	if err := scanner.Err(); err != nil {
		fmt.Println("Error reading file:", err)
	}
}
```

```go
func processLine(line string) {
    fmt.Println("Processing:", line) // Replace with actual processing
}
```

✔ Uses bufio.Scanner to read files line by line, avoiding memory overload.

16.4.2 Using Goroutines for Parallel Processing

When processing large datasets, using goroutines allows tasks to run concurrently.

Example: Processing Data Concurrently

go

CopyEdit

```go
import (
    "fmt"
    "sync"
)

func processChunk(id int, data []int, wg *sync.WaitGroup) {
    defer wg.Done()
    fmt.Printf("Worker %d processing %d items\n", id, len(data))
}

func main() {
```

```
data := make([]int, 100000)

chunkSize := 10000

var wg sync.WaitGroup


for i := 0; i < len(data); i += chunkSize {

  end := i + chunkSize

  if end > len(data) {

    end = len(data)

  }


  wg.Add(1)

  go processChunk(i/chunkSize, data[i:end], &wg)

}


wg.Wait()

fmt.Println("All chunks processed")

}
```

✔ Splits large datasets into smaller chunks and processes them in parallel.

16.4.3 Using Batching to Reduce Database Load

Instead of inserting one row at a time, batch insertions improve database performance.

Example: Batch Inserting Data

go

CopyEdit

```go
import (
    "database/sql"

    "fmt"

    "log"


    _ "github.com/lib/pq"
)


func batchInsert(db *sql.DB, users []User) {
    query := "INSERT INTO users (name, email) VALUES "

    values := []interface{}{}

    placeholders := ""


    for i, user := range users {
        placeholders += fmt.Sprintf("($%d, $%d),", i*2+1, i*2+2)

        values = append(values, user.Name, user.Email)
```

```go
    }

    query += placeholders[:len(placeholders)-1] // Remove trailing comma

    _, err := db.Exec(query, values...)
    if err != nil {
        log.Fatal("Error inserting batch:", err)
    }
}

type User struct {
    Name  string
    Email string
}

func main() {
    dsn := "user=postgres password=secret dbname=mydb sslmode=disable"
    db, err := sql.Open("postgres", dsn)
    if err != nil {
        log.Fatal(err)
    }
    defer db.Close()
```

```go
users := []User{
    {"Alice", "alice@example.com"},
    {"Bob", "bob@example.com"},
}

batchInsert(db, users)
fmt.Println("Batch insert successful")
}
```

✔ Uses batch inserts to reduce database overhead.

16.4.4 Using Efficient JSON Streaming

When dealing with large JSON responses, process them in chunks instead of loading everything into memory.

Example: Streaming Large JSON Responses

go

CopyEdit

```go
import (
    "encoding/json"
    "fmt"
    "net/http"
```

```go
)

type User struct {
    ID    int    `json:"id"`
    Name  string `json:"name"`
    Email string `json:"email"`
}

func streamJSONResponse(w http.ResponseWriter, r *http.Request) {
    users := []User{
        {1, "Alice", "alice@example.com"},
        {2, "Bob", "bob@example.com"},
    }

    w.Header().Set("Content-Type", "application/json")
    encoder := json.NewEncoder(w)

    w.Write([]byte("["))
    for i, user := range users {
        if i > 0 {
            w.Write([]byte(","))
        }
```

```go
        encoder.Encode(user)

    }

    w.Write([]byte("]"))

}


func main() {

    http.HandleFunc("/users", streamJSONResponse)

    http.ListenAndServe(":8080", nil)

}
```

✔ Streams JSON data instead of loading it all at once into memory.

16.4.5 Caching Frequently Accessed Data

Frequent database queries slow down performance. Use in-memory caching (Redis, Go maps) to store precomputed data.

Example: Using a Go Map for In-Memory Caching

go

CopyEdit

```go
var cache = make(map[string]string)


func getCachedValue(key string) string {

    if val, found := cache[key]; found {
```

```
    return val
  }

  cache[key] = "computed-value" // Simulate expensive computation

  return cache[key]

}
```

✔ Avoids redundant database queries by caching results.

✔ Use pprof for profiling CPU and memory usage.
✔ Process large files using streaming (bufio.Scanner).
✔ Optimize database operations with batch inserts and caching.
✔ Use goroutines for concurrent data processing.
✔ Stream large JSON responses instead of loading them all into memory.

Chapter 17: Deploying Go Applications

Go is known for its **efficient compilation, portability, and ease of deployment**, making it an excellent choice for deploying applications across different platforms. One of Go's biggest advantages is that it can **compile a single binary executable**, eliminating the need for external dependencies. This chapter covers **cross-compiling for multiple operating systems, packaging Go applications**, and **distributing them effectively**.

17.1 Compiling Go Applications for Different Platforms

Go's compiler supports **cross-compilation**, allowing developers to build binaries for different operating systems and architectures from a single machine.

17.1.1 Understanding Go Compilation

Go applications compile into a **standalone binary** that contains all necessary dependencies. This means:

■ No need for separate runtime dependencies
■ Faster startup times
■ Easier deployment (single binary)

Go compiles code using:

sh
CopyEdit
```
go build -o myapp main.go
```

✔ **Generates a binary (myapp) that runs on the host OS.**

17.1.2 Cross-Compiling for Other Operating Systems

Go supports cross-compilation via GOOS (target OS) and GOARCH (target architecture).

OS	GOOS Value
Windows	windows
macOS	darwin
Linux	linux
FreeBSD	freebsd

Architecture	GOARCH Value
AMD64 (64-bit)	amd64
ARM 32-bit	arm
ARM 64-bit	arm64
Intel 386	386

Example: Cross-Compile for Windows from Linux/macOS

sh
CopyEdit
```
GOOS=windows GOARCH=amd64 go build -o myapp.exe main.go
```

✔ Generates a myapp.exe binary for Windows.

Example: Cross-Compile for Linux from macOS

sh
CopyEdit
```
GOOS=linux GOARCH=amd64 go build -o myapp-linux main.go
```

✔ Creates a Linux binary (myapp-linux).

Example: Cross-Compile for macOS from Linux

sh
CopyEdit
```
GOOS=darwin GOARCH=amd64 go build -o myapp-mac main.go
```

✔ **Builds a macOS executable (myapp-mac).**

17.1.3 Building for Multiple Platforms at Once

To **automate cross-compilation**, use a script:

sh
CopyEdit
```bash
#!/bin/bash

PLATFORMS=("windows/amd64" "linux/amd64" "darwin/amd64")

for PLATFORM in "${PLATFORMS[@]}"; do
  GOOS=${PLATFORM%/*}
  GOARCH=${PLATFORM#*/}
  OUTPUT="myapp-$GOOS-$GOARCH"

  if [ "$GOOS" == "windows" ]; then
    OUTPUT+=".exe"
  fi

  echo "Building for $GOOS/$GOARCH..."
  GOOS=$GOOS GOARCH=$GOARCH go build -o $OUTPUT main.go
done

echo "Builds complete!"
```

✔ **Generates binaries for Windows, Linux, and macOS with one command.**

Run:

```sh
CopyEdit
chmod +x build.sh
./build.sh
```

17.1.4 Stripping and Compressing Binaries

Go binaries can be **large** due to debugging symbols. Use strip to reduce size:

```sh
CopyEdit
strip myapp
```

✔ **Removes unnecessary debug symbols.**

For further size reduction, use upx:

```sh
CopyEdit
upx --best myapp
```

✔ **Compresses the binary while keeping it executable.**

17.1.5 Building a Static Binary

For **fully standalone binaries**, disable CGO (C-based dependencies):

```sh
CopyEdit
CGO_ENABLED=0 GOOS=linux GOARCH=amd64 go build -o myapp-static main.go
```

✔ **Ensures no external dependencies are required.**

17.2 Packaging and Distributing Go Applications

Once compiled, Go applications can be **packaged and distributed** in different ways.

17.2.1 Creating a Tarball for Distribution

The simplest method is to package the binary into a compressed tarball:

```sh
CopyEdit
tar -czvf myapp-linux.tar.gz myapp
```

✔ **Bundles the binary for easy distribution.**

17.2.2 Creating a Debian Package (.deb)

For **Debian/Ubuntu**, package the binary as a .deb file:

1. Create necessary folders:

```sh
CopyEdit
mkdir -p myapp-deb/DEBIAN
mkdir -p myapp-deb/usr/local/bin
```

2. Create a control file (myapp-deb/DEBIAN/control):

```vbnet
CopyEdit
Package: myapp
Version: 1.0
Section: base
Priority: optional
```

Architecture: amd64
Maintainer: Your Name <your@email.com>
Description: My awesome Go app

3 Copy the binary:

sh
CopyEdit

```
cp myapp myapp-deb/usr/local/bin/
```

4 Build the package:

sh
CopyEdit

```
dpkg-deb --build myapp-deb
```

✔ **Creates myapp-deb.deb, which can be installed using dpkg -i myapp-deb.deb.**

17.2.3 Creating an RPM Package (.rpm)

For **RedHat-based systems** (CentOS, Fedora), use rpmbuild:

1 Install rpm-build:

sh
CopyEdit

```
sudo yum install rpm-build
```

2 Create necessary folders:

sh
CopyEdit

```
mkdir -p ~/rpmbuild/{BUILD,RPMS,SOURCES,SPECS,SRPMS}
```

3 Create a spec file (~/rpmbuild/SPECS/myapp.spec):

perl
CopyEdit
```
Name: myapp
Version: 1.0
Release: 1%{?dist}
Summary: My Go application
License: MIT
Source0: myapp.tar.gz

%description
A simple Go application.

%prep

%install
mkdir -p %{buildroot}/usr/local/bin
install -m 755 %{SOURCE0} %{buildroot}/usr/local/bin/myapp

%files
/usr/local/bin/myapp

%changelog
```

4 Build the RPM package:

sh
CopyEdit
```
rpmbuild -ba ~/rpmbuild/SPECS/myapp.spec
```

✔ **Creates an .rpm package for installation.**

17.2.4 Creating a Docker Image for Distribution

Docker simplifies application deployment by **packaging the app with its dependencies**.

Create a Dockerfile
dockerfile
CopyEdit

```
FROM golang:1.20 AS builder

WORKDIR /app
COPY . .
RUN go build -o myapp

FROM alpine:latest
WORKDIR /root/
COPY --from=builder /app/myapp .
CMD ["./myapp"]
```

✔ **Builds the Go binary inside a minimal Docker container.**

Build and Run the Docker Image
sh
CopyEdit

```
docker build -t myapp .
docker run --rm myapp
```

✔ **Creates a portable, self-contained application image.**

17.2.5 Distributing Go Applications via GitHub Releases

Automate builds and releases using GitHub Actions.

1️⃣ **Create a release tag:**

```sh
CopyEdit
git tag -a v1.0 -m "Version 1.0"
git push origin v1.0
```

2️⃣ **Upload binaries to GitHub Releases:**

```sh
CopyEdit
gh release create v1.0 myapp-linux.tar.gz myapp-windows.zip --notes "Initial release"
```

✔ **Publishes the binaries for easy download.**

17.2.6 Publishing Go Applications to Homebrew

For macOS users, publish Go applications to **Homebrew**.

1️⃣ Fork **homebrew-core** repository.
2️⃣ Create a formula (myapp.rb):

```ruby
CopyEdit
class Myapp < Formula
  desc "My awesome Go app"
  homepage "https://github.com/username/myapp"
  url "https://github.com/username/myapp/releases/download/v1.0/myapp-mac.tar.gz"
  sha256 "checksum"

  def install
    bin.install "myapp"
```

```
end
    end
```

3 Submit a pull request to **Homebrew/homebrew-core**.

✔ **Users can install your app via** brew install myapp.

✔ **Go enables cross-platform compilation with** GOOS **and** GOARCH.

✔ **Package applications as** .tar.gz, .deb, .rpm, **or Docker images.**

✔ **Use GitHub Releases and Homebrew for easy distribution.**

✔ **Docker simplifies deployment by bundling everything in one container.**

Deploying Go applications to cloud platforms like AWS, DigitalOcean, and Heroku ensures high availability and scalability. Go applications can be easily containerized using Docker, making deployments more consistent across different environments.

This chapter covers deploying Go apps on AWS, DigitalOcean, and Heroku, along with Dockerizing Go applications for production use.

17.3 Deploying Go Apps on AWS, DigitalOcean, and Heroku

Go applications can be deployed on AWS, DigitalOcean, and Heroku using various methods like bare metal servers (EC2, Droplets), containerized deployments (ECS, Kubernetes), or fully managed services like Elastic Beanstalk.

17.3.1 Deploying Go Apps on AWS

AWS offers multiple ways to deploy Go applications:

■ **EC2 Instances – Directly host the Go binary on a virtual machine.**

■ **Elastic Beanstalk – Simplifies deployment by managing infrastructure automatically.**

■ **ECS (Elastic Container Service)** – Uses Docker containers for deployment.
■ **Lambda (Serverless)** – Run Go functions without managing servers.

Deploying a Go App on AWS EC2

☐1 Launch an EC2 instance

- Use Amazon Linux or Ubuntu.
- Allow port 80 or 443 for web applications.

☐2 Install Go and Deploy the App

sh

CopyEdit

```
sudo yum update -y

sudo yum install -y golang
```

☐3 Transfer the Go binary to EC2
On your local machine, compile for Linux:

sh

CopyEdit

```
GOOS=linux GOARCH=amd64 go build -o myapp main.go

scp -i your-key.pem myapp ec2-user@your-ec2-instance:/home/ec2-user/
```

4 Run the Go Application

sh

CopyEdit

```
chmod +x myapp

./myapp
```

✔ **Your application is now running on AWS EC2!**

Deploying a Go App on AWS Elastic Beanstalk

AWS Elastic Beanstalk automates deployment, scaling, and infrastructure management.

1 Install the Elastic Beanstalk CLI

sh

CopyEdit

```
pip install awsebcli --upgrade
```

2 Initialize a New Elastic Beanstalk App

sh

CopyEdit

```
eb init -p go go-app
```

3 Deploy the Application

sh

CopyEdit

eb create go-app-env

✔ Elastic Beanstalk provisions infrastructure and deploys your Go app automatically.

Deploying a Go App on DigitalOcean

DigitalOcean provides Droplets (VMs) and App Platform (Managed PaaS) for Go applications.

Deploying on a DigitalOcean Droplet (VM)

1 Create a Droplet with Ubuntu.
2 SSH into the Droplet

sh

CopyEdit

ssh root@your-droplet-ip

3 Install Go and Deploy the App

sh

CopyEdit

sudo apt update && sudo apt install -y golang

scp myapp root@your-droplet-ip:/root/

```
chmod +x myapp

./myapp
```

✔ Your app is now running on DigitalOcean!

Deploying a Go App on Heroku

Heroku is a Platform-as-a-Service (PaaS) that makes Go deployments simple.

1 Install the Heroku CLI

sh

CopyEdit

```
curl https://cli-assets.heroku.com/install.sh | sh
```

2 Login and Create a New Heroku App

sh

CopyEdit

```
heroku login
heroku create my-go-app
```

3 Deploy the Application

sh

CopyEdit

```
git init
```

288

```
heroku git:remote -a my-go-app

echo "web: ./myapp" > Procfile

git add .

git commit -m "Deploy Go app"

git push heroku main
```

✔ Heroku automatically builds and runs your Go application.

17.4 Dockerizing Go Applications for Production

Dockerizing a Go application ensures that it runs consistently across different environments.

17.4.1 Writing a Dockerfile for a Go App

A Dockerfile defines the environment needed to run a Go application inside a container.

Minimal Dockerfile for a Go Web App

dockerfile

CopyEdit

```
# Build Stage

FROM golang:1.20 AS builder


WORKDIR /app
```

```
COPY . .

RUN go build -o myapp


# Deployment Stage

FROM alpine:latest

WORKDIR /root/

COPY --from=builder /app/myapp .

CMD ["./myapp"]
```

✔ Uses a multi-stage build to reduce image size.
✔ Copies only the compiled binary, making it lightweight.

17.4.2 Building and Running the Docker Container

1️⃣ Build the Docker Image

sh

CopyEdit

```
docker build -t myapp .
```


2️⃣ Run the Container Locally

sh

CopyEdit

```
docker run -p 8080:8080 myapp
```

✔ **Your Go app is now running inside Docker!**

17.4.3 Running the Container in Production

Deploying on AWS ECS

[1] **Push the Docker Image to AWS ECR**

sh

CopyEdit

```
aws ecr create-repository --repository-name myapp

docker tag myapp:latest <aws-ecr-url>/myapp:latest

docker push <aws-ecr-url>/myapp:latest
```

[2] **Deploy to AWS ECS**

sh

CopyEdit

```
aws ecs create-cluster --cluster-name go-cluster

aws ecs create-service --cluster go-cluster --service-name go-service
--task-definition go-task
```

✔ **Runs the Docker container in AWS ECS.**

Deploying on DigitalOcean App Platform

1 Push to DigitalOcean Container Registry

sh

CopyEdit

```
doctl registry login

docker tag myapp registry.digitalocean.com/myapp:latest

docker push registry.digitalocean.com/myapp:latest
```

2 Deploy Using DigitalOcean App Platform

sh

CopyEdit

```
doctl apps create --spec app.yaml
```

✔ Your Dockerized Go app is now live on DigitalOcean!

Deploying on Kubernetes

For Kubernetes (GKE, EKS, AKS):

1 Create a Deployment YAML

yaml

CopyEdit

```
apiVersion: apps/v1

kind: Deployment
```

```yaml
metadata:
  name: go-app
spec:
  replicas: 2
  selector:
    matchLabels:
      app: go-app
  template:
    metadata:
      labels:
        app: go-app
    spec:
      containers:
      - name: go-app
        image: myapp:latest
        ports:
        - containerPort: 8080
```

2 Deploy to Kubernetes

sh

CopyEdit

kubectl apply -f deployment.yaml

✔ Runs the Dockerized Go application on Kubernetes.

17.4.4 Pushing Docker Images to Docker Hub

1️⃣ Login to Docker Hub

sh

CopyEdit

```
docker login
```

2️⃣ Tag and Push the Image

sh

CopyEdit

```
docker tag myapp username/myapp:latest

docker push username/myapp:latest
```

✔ Users can now pull and run your Go app via Docker Hub.

✔ Go applications can be deployed on AWS, DigitalOcean, and Heroku easily.
✔ Dockerizing Go apps ensures portability and consistency across environments.
✔ Deploy Docker containers using ECS, Kubernetes, or DigitalOcean App Platform.
✔ Publishing Docker images to Docker Hub allows easy distribution.

Chapter 18: Using Go in Microservices

Microservices architecture is a modern approach to building scalable, modular applications by breaking them into **small, independently deployable services**. Go is an **excellent choice** for microservices due to its **high performance, lightweight concurrency, and easy deployment**.

This chapter covers **the fundamentals of microservices architecture**, and provides a **detailed guide to building a microservice in Go**.

18.1 Understanding Microservices Architecture

Microservices architecture is a **decentralized approach** where an application is divided into smaller services that communicate via APIs. Each service is responsible for a **single functionality** and operates independently.

18.1.1 Key Characteristics of Microservices

- **Single Responsibility** – Each service focuses on one business function.
- **Independently Deployable** – Services can be updated and scaled separately.
- **Communication via APIs** – Services communicate using **RESTful APIs or gRPC**.
- **Decentralized Data Management** – Each service can use its own database.
- **Scalability** – Can scale individual services based on demand.

18.1.2 Microservices vs Monolithic Architecture

Feature	Monolithic	Microservices
Deployment	Single unit	Independent services
Scalability	Scales as a whole	Scales per service
Code Maintainability	Can be complex	Easier to manage
Data Storage	Single database	Separate DB per service
Technology Stack	Limited flexibility	Can mix technologies

✔ Microservices allow better scaling and flexibility, whereas monoliths are easier to start with.

18.1.3 When to Use Microservices

■ For large applications that require scaling different parts independently.
■ When teams need to develop, test, and deploy services separately.
■ For applications requiring high availability and resilience.
■ When different services require different technology stacks.

🔔 Avoid microservices if:

- The application is small and doesn't require independent scaling.
- The team lacks experience in managing distributed systems.

18.2 Building a Microservice in Go

Go is a great language for microservices due to its **fast execution, efficient concurrency, and small binary size**.

18.2.1 Setting Up a Simple Microservice

We'll create a **User Microservice** using **Gin** (for API handling) and **GORM** (for database interactions).

Install Dependencies
sh
CopyEdit
```
go get -u github.com/gin-gonic/gin
go get -u gorm.io/gorm gorm.io/driver/sqlite
```

18.2.2 Defining the User Model

Each microservice typically **has its own database**. We will use **SQLite** in this example.

go
CopyEdit
```go
package main

import (
    "gorm.io/driver/sqlite"
    "gorm.io/gorm"
    "log"
)

var db *gorm.DB

type User struct {
    ID    uint   `gorm:"primaryKey"`
    Name  string `json:"name"`
    Email string `gorm:"unique" json:"email"`
}

func initDB() {
    var err error
    db, err = gorm.Open(sqlite.Open("users.db"), &gorm.Config{})
    if err != nil {
        log.Fatal("Failed to connect to database:", err)
    }

    db.AutoMigrate(&User{}) // Create table if not exists
}
```

✔ **Each microservice has its own database and model.**
✔ **Uses gorm.Open(sqlite.Open("users.db")) to manage data storage.**

18.2.3 Implementing CRUD Operations

Microservices expose **RESTful endpoints** to allow interaction with their data.

Creating a User (POST /users)

go
CopyEdit

```go
import "github.com/gin-gonic/gin"

func createUser(c *gin.Context) {
    var user User
    if err := c.ShouldBindJSON(&user); err != nil {
        c.JSON(400, gin.H{"error": "Invalid request"})
        return
    }

    db.Create(&user)
    c.JSON(201, gin.H{"message": "User created", "user": user})
}
```

✔ c.ShouldBindJSON(&user) **parses incoming JSON request.**
✔ **Uses** db.Create(&user) **to insert data into the database.**

Fetching All Users (GET /users)

go
CopyEdit

```go
func getUsers(c *gin.Context) {
    var users []User
    db.Find(&users)
    c.JSON(200, users)
}
```

✔ **Returns all users in JSON format.**

Fetching a User by ID (GET /users/:id)

go
CopyEdit
```go
func getUserByID(c *gin.Context) {
    id := c.Param("id")
    var user User

    if err := db.First(&user, id).Error; err != nil {
        c.JSON(404, gin.H{"error": "User not found"})
        return
    }

    c.JSON(200, user)
}
```

✔ Uses db.First(&user, id) to fetch a user by ID.

Updating a User (PUT /users/:id)

go
CopyEdit
```go
func updateUser(c *gin.Context) {
    id := c.Param("id")
    var user User

    if err := db.First(&user, id).Error; err != nil {
        c.JSON(404, gin.H{"error": "User not found"})
        return
    }

    if err := c.ShouldBindJSON(&user); err != nil {
        c.JSON(400, gin.H{"error": "Invalid input"})
        return
    }

    db.Save(&user)
```

```
c.JSON(200, gin.H{"message": "User updated", "user": user})
}
```

✔ **Updates user details using** db.Save(&user).

Deleting a User (DELETE /users/:id)

go
CopyEdit
```
func deleteUser(c *gin.Context) {
    id := c.Param("id")
    var user User

    if err := db.First(&user, id).Error; err != nil {
        c.JSON(404, gin.H{"error": "User not found"})
        return
    }

    db.Delete(&user)
    c.JSON(200, gin.H{"message": "User deleted"})
}
```

✔ **Deletes a user using** db.Delete(&user).

18.2.4 Registering API Routes

Finally, set up the API routes and run the service.

go
CopyEdit
```
func main() {
    initDB()
    r := gin.Default()

    r.POST("/users", createUser)
```

```
r.GET("/users", getUsers)
r.GET("/users/:id", getUserByID)
r.PUT("/users/:id", updateUser)
r.DELETE("/users/:id", deleteUser)

r.Run(":8080") // Start the server on port 8080
}
```

✔ **Runs the microservice on** localhost:8080.

18.2.5 Running and Testing the Microservice

Run the service:

sh
CopyEdit
```
go run main.go
```

Test it using **curl**:

■ **Create a User**

sh
CopyEdit
```
curl -X POST http://localhost:8080/users -d
'{"name":"Alice","email":"alice@example.com"}' -H "Content-Type: application/json"
```

■ **Get All Users**

sh
CopyEdit
```
curl -X GET http://localhost:8080/users
```

✔ Microservices break applications into independent services for better scalability.
✔ Go is well-suited for microservices due to its concurrency, efficiency, and deployment simplicity.
✔ Each microservice should have its own database to ensure loose coupling.
✔ APIs expose CRUD functionality for external communication

Once we have individual microservices, we need to ensure efficient communication between them, manage traffic, and monitor performance. API Gateways help in routing, load balancing, authentication, and security, while monitoring and scaling tools ensure high availability and reliability.

This section covers API gateways, service-to-service communication, monitoring, and scaling strategies for Go microservices.

18.3 API Gateway and Service Communication

18.3.1 What is an API Gateway?

An API Gateway is a single entry point that routes requests to different microservices. It acts as a reverse proxy, improving security, scalability, and efficiency.

■ Manages all API requests – Routes requests to appropriate microservices.
■ Handles authentication & authorization – Verifies API tokens (JWT, OAuth).
■ Performs load balancing – Distributes requests across multiple service instances.
■ Reduces network overhead – Aggregates responses from multiple services.

18.3.2 Popular API Gateway Solutions

Gateway	Key Features
Kong	Open-source, extensible, built-in security
Traefik	Lightweight, auto-discovers services
NGINX	High-performance, flexible routing
AWS API Gateway	Fully managed, integrates with AWS Lambda
Envoy	Built-in service discovery, great for Kubernetes

18.3.3 Implementing an API Gateway with Nginx

Step 1: Install Nginx

sh

CopyEdit

sudo apt update && sudo apt install nginx -y

Step 2: Configure Nginx as an API Gateway

Edit the Nginx configuration file (/etc/nginx/sites-available/api_gateway):

nginx

CopyEdit

```
server {
    listen 80;

    location /users/ {
        proxy_pass http://localhost:8080/;
```

```
    }

    location /orders/ {

        proxy_pass http://localhost:8081/;

    }

}
```

✔ Requests to /users/ are routed to the User service (:8080).
✔ Requests to /orders/ are routed to the Order service (:8081).

Step 3: Enable and Restart Nginx

sh

CopyEdit

sudo ln -s /etc/nginx/sites-available/api_gateway /etc/nginx/sites-enabled/

sudo systemctl restart nginx

Now, requests to http://yourdomain.com/users/ are automatically routed to the
User Service.

18.3.4 Service-to-Service Communication with gRPC

Microservices need to communicate efficiently. gRPC is a high-performance RPC framework that uses Protocol Buffers (protobufs) for serialization.

Installing gRPC in Go

sh

CopyEdit

```sh
go get google.golang.org/grpc

go get google.golang.org/protobuf
```

Defining a gRPC Service (user.proto)

proto

CopyEdit

```proto
syntax = "proto3";


service UserService {
    rpc GetUser (UserRequest) returns (UserResponse);
}


message UserRequest {
    string id = 1;
}
```

```
message UserResponse {

    string id = 1;

    string name = 2;

    string email = 3;

}
```

Generating gRPC Code

sh

CopyEdit

```
protoc --go_out=. --go-grpc_out=. user.proto
```

✔ **Converts** .proto **files into Go code for communication.**

Implementing a gRPC Server

go

CopyEdit

```
type userService struct{}


func (s *userService) GetUser(ctx context.Context, req *pb.UserRequest)
(*pb.UserResponse, error) {

    return &pb.UserResponse{

        Id:   req.Id,
```

```
    Name:  "Alice",

    Email: "alice@example.com",

  }, nil

}
```

✔ Allows internal services to communicate efficiently using gRPC.

18.4 Monitoring and Scaling Microservices

18.4.1 Why Monitoring is Important

Monitoring helps detect performance bottlenecks, downtime, and errors in microservices.

■ Detects service failures – Monitors response times and error rates.
■ Tracks resource usage – CPU, memory, and network consumption.
■ Provides real-time alerts – Notifies developers of system failures.

18.4.2 Using Prometheus for Monitoring

Prometheus is a popular metrics collection tool for microservices.

Step 1: Install Prometheus

sh

CopyEdit

```
wget
https://github.com/prometheus/prometheus/releases/latest/download/prometheus-li
nux-amd64.tar.gz

tar -xvzf prometheus-linux-amd64.tar.gz
```

```sh
cd prometheus-linux-amd64

./prometheus --config.file=prometheus.yml
```

Step 2: Expose Metrics in a Go Service

Use Prometheus client library:

sh

CopyEdit

```sh
go get github.com/prometheus/client_golang/prometheus

go get github.com/prometheus/client_golang/prometheus/promhttp
```

Step 3: Add Metrics to Go Microservice

go

CopyEdit

```go
import (

    "github.com/prometheus/client_golang/prometheus"

    "github.com/prometheus/client_golang/prometheus/promhttp"

    "net/http"

)


var requestCount = prometheus.NewCounter(

    prometheus.CounterOpts{

        Name: "user_requests_total",
```

```go
        Help: "Total number of user service requests",
    },
)


func init() {
    prometheus.MustRegister(requestCount)
}


func userHandler(w http.ResponseWriter, r *http.Request) {
    requestCount.Inc() // Increase request count metric
    w.Write([]byte("User service is running"))
}


func main() {
    http.Handle("/metrics", promhttp.Handler())
    http.HandleFunc("/user", userHandler)
    http.ListenAndServe(":8080", nil)
}
```

✔ **Metrics available at** http://localhost:8080/metrics.

18.4.3 Scaling Microservices with Kubernetes

Kubernetes is a container orchestration platform for scaling and managing microservices.

Step 1: Create a Kubernetes Deployment

yaml

CopyEdit

```yaml
apiVersion: apps/v1
kind: Deployment
metadata:
  name: user-service
spec:
  replicas: 3
  selector:
    matchLabels:
      app: user-service
  template:
    metadata:
      labels:
        app: user-service
    spec:
      containers:
      - name: user-service
```

```
image: myrepo/user-service:latest

ports:

- containerPort: 8080
```

✔ **Runs 3 instances of the User Service.**

Step 2: Create a Kubernetes Service

yaml

CopyEdit

```
apiVersion: v1

kind: Service

metadata:

  name: user-service

spec:

  selector:

    app: user-service

  ports:

    - protocol: TCP

      port: 80

      targetPort: 8080
```

✔ **Exposes the User Service via a load balancer.**

Step 3: Deploy to Kubernetes

sh

CopyEdit

```
kubectl apply -f deployment.yaml

kubectl apply -f service.yaml
```

✔ **Microservices are now running in Kubernetes with automatic scaling.**

18.4.4 Load Balancing Microservices

Use NGINX or Kubernetes Ingress Controller to balance traffic.

Example: Load Balancer for User Service

nginx

CopyEdit

```
upstream users {

    server user-service-1:8080;

    server user-service-2:8080;

    server user-service-3:8080;

}


server {

    listen 80;

    location /users/ {
```

```
    proxy_pass http://users;

}

}
```

✔ Evenly distributes requests among multiple service instances.

✔ API Gateways simplify routing and security.
✔ gRPC enables high-performance microservice communication.
✔ Prometheus monitors service health and performance.
✔ Kubernetes scales microservices automatically.
✔ Load balancers distribute traffic efficiently

Chapter 19: Final Capstone Project – Building a Full-Stack Go Application

In this chapter, we will **apply everything we've learned** to build a **complete full-stack Go application**. This project will include a **backend API with Go**, a **frontend client**, and a **database layer**. We will also cover **best practices for structuring a Go application, handling authentication**, and **deploying the final application**.

19.1 Project Overview: A Complete Web App or API

19.1.1 What We Will Build

For this capstone project, we will build a **Full-Stack Task Management Application** with the following features:

- **User Authentication** – Sign up, login, JWT-based authentication.
- **Task Management** – Create, update, delete, and list tasks.
- **Database Integration** – Store users and tasks in PostgreSQL.
- **API Development** – A RESTful backend using Go and Gin.
- **Frontend with React** – A modern UI built with React.js.
- **Dockerized Deployment** – Deployable with Docker & Kubernetes.

19.1.2 Tech Stack

Component	Technology
Backend API	Go + Gin
Frontend	React.js (or optional Vue.js)
Database	PostgreSQL
Authentication	JWT (JSON Web Tokens)
Deployment	Docker, Kubernetes (optional)
API Docs	Swagger/OpenAPI

19.2 Designing the Project Architecture

19.2.1 High-Level System Design

Our task management app will follow a **modular architecture** with the following key components:

■ **Frontend (React.js)** – Calls the backend API to display tasks and manage user interactions.
■ **Backend (Go + Gin)** – Handles authentication, task management, and database operations.
■ **Database (PostgreSQL)** – Stores user and task data.
■ **API Gateway (Optional)** – Handles routing and authentication for microservices.

19.2.2 Project Folder Structure

A well-structured Go project follows **clean architecture principles** to keep the code **maintainable and scalable**.

```
go
CopyEdit
task-manager/
│── backend/
│   │── main.go
│   │── config/
│   │   └── config.go
│   │── controllers/
│   │   ├── auth_controller.go
│   │   ├── task_controller.go
│   │── models/
│   │   ├── user.go
│   │   ├── task.go
│   │── routes/
│   │   ├── auth_routes.go
│   │   ├── task_routes.go
│   │── middleware/
│   │   ├── jwt_middleware.go
```

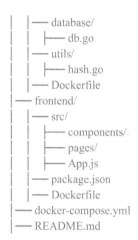

```
|   |── database/
|   |   ├── db.go
|   |── utils/
|   |   ├── hash.go
|   |── Dockerfile
|── frontend/
|   |── src/
|   |   ├── components/
|   |   ├── pages/
|   |   ├── App.js
|   |── package.json
|   |── Dockerfile
|── docker-compose.yml
|── README.md
```

19.2.3 Backend API Design

The backend will expose **RESTful API endpoints**.

Method	Endpoint	Description
POST	/api/auth/register	Register a new user
POST	/api/auth/login	Login and get JWT token
GET	/api/tasks	Get all tasks (Authenticated)
POST	/api/tasks	Create a new task
PUT	/api/tasks/:id	Update a task
DELETE	/api/tasks/:id	Delete a task

19.2.4 Database Schema (PostgreSQL)

Users Table
sql
CopyEdit
CREATE TABLE users (
    id SERIAL PRIMARY KEY,

316

```sql
name VARCHAR(50) NOT NULL,
email VARCHAR(100) UNIQUE NOT NULL,
password TEXT NOT NULL
);
```

Tasks Table

sql
CopyEdit
```sql
CREATE TABLE tasks (
    id SERIAL PRIMARY KEY,
    user_id INTEGER REFERENCES users(id),
    title VARCHAR(100) NOT NULL,
    description TEXT,
    status VARCHAR(20) DEFAULT 'pending',
    created_at TIMESTAMP DEFAULT NOW(),
    updated_at TIMESTAMP DEFAULT NOW()
);
```

19.2.5 Authentication & Security Design

- **JWT Authentication**: Users will receive a **JWT token** upon login, which will be required for accessing protected routes.
- **Middleware**: All requests will pass through **JWT validation middleware** before reaching task endpoints.
- **Password Hashing**: User passwords will be **hashed using bcrypt** before storing them in the database.

JWT-Based Authentication Flow

1. **User Registers** → Sends POST /api/auth/register
2. **User Logs In** → Gets JWT token from POST /api/auth/login
3. **User Requests Tasks** → Sends token in Authorization: Bearer <token> header
4. **Backend Verifies JWT** → Decodes token, checks validity, processes request

---

19.2.6 Frontend UI Design (React.js)

The **React frontend** will include:
- **Login & Signup Pages**
- **Task Dashboard** – Displays a list of tasks
- **Task Actions** – Add, edit, delete tasks
- **Protected Routes** – Only accessible with a valid JWT token

React Routes

Route	Page
/login	Login Page
/register	Register Page
/tasks	Task List (Protected)
/tasks/new	Add Task Page
/tasks/edit/:id	Edit Task Page

19.2.7 Deployment Strategy

1 Dockerized Deployment

Each component (backend & frontend) will be **containerized** using Docker.
- **Dockerfile for Backend**
- **Dockerfile for Frontend**
- **Docker Compose for Local Development**

2 Cloud Deployment Options

- **AWS ECS / DigitalOcean App Platform** – For scalable deployments
- **Heroku** – For quick and free deployment
- **Kubernetes** – For highly scalable microservice deployment

19.2.8 Example Docker Compose File

To run the full-stack application **locally** with PostgreSQL, we will use Docker Compose:

```yaml
yaml
CopyEdit
version: "3.8"

services:
  backend:
    build: ./backend
    ports:
      - "8080:8080"
    depends_on:
      - db
    environment:
      - DB_HOST=db
      - DB_USER=postgres
      - DB_PASSWORD=secret
      - DB_NAME=taskdb

  frontend:
    build: ./frontend
    ports:
      - "3000:3000"
    depends_on:
      - backend

  db:
    image: postgres:latest
    restart: always
    environment:
      POSTGRES_USER: postgres
      POSTGRES_PASSWORD: secret
      POSTGRES_DB: taskdb
    ports:
      - "5432:5432"
```

✔ This setup runs PostgreSQL, the Go backend, and the React frontend together.

✔ We designed a full-stack application with authentication, CRUD functionality, and security.
✔ The backend follows clean architecture principles.
✔ The frontend is a modern UI with React.js.
✔ The project is fully Dockerized for deployment.
✔ It can be deployed on AWS, DigitalOcean, or Kubernetes.

In this section, we will implement the core features of our Task Management App, test and debug it, and deploy it online for real-world use.

19.3 Implementing Features and Business Logic

Our backend will include:

■ User Authentication – Register, login, JWT authentication.
■ Task Management – CRUD operations for tasks.
■ Middleware – Secure routes with JWT-based authentication.
■ Database Integration – Store users and tasks in PostgreSQL.
■ Logging and Error Handling – Debugging-friendly logs and structured error messages.

19.3.1 Implementing User Authentication (Register & Login)

User Model (models/user.go)

go

CopyEdit

```go
package models

import "gorm.io/gorm"

type User struct {
    ID       uint   `gorm:"primaryKey"`
    Name     string `json:"name"`
    Email    string `gorm:"unique" json:"email"`
    Password string `json:"password"`
}
```

Hashing Passwords (utils/hash.go)

go

CopyEdit

```go
package utils

import "golang.org/x/crypto/bcrypt"
```

321

```go
func HashPassword(password string) (string, error) {

    bytes, err := bcrypt.GenerateFromPassword([]byte(password),
bcrypt.DefaultCost)

    return string(bytes), err

}


func CheckPasswordHash(password, hash string) bool {

    return bcrypt.CompareHashAndPassword([]byte(hash), []byte(password)) == nil

}
```

✔ Ensures passwords are securely hashed before storing.

Registering a User (controllers/auth_controller.go)

go

CopyEdit

```go
package controllers


import (

    "myapp/models"

    "myapp/utils"

    "gorm.io/gorm"

    "github.com/gin-gonic/gin"
```

```go
    "net/http"
)


var db *gorm.DB


func Register(c *gin.Context) {
    var input models.User
    if err := c.ShouldBindJSON(&input); err != nil {
        c.JSON(http.StatusBadRequest, gin.H{"error": "Invalid input"})
        return
    }


    hashedPassword, _ := utils.HashPassword(input.Password)
    input.Password = hashedPassword


    db.Create(&input)
    c.JSON(http.StatusCreated, gin.H{"message": "User registered successfully"})
}
```

✔ **Validates user input and stores a hashed password.**

Login & JWT Generation (controllers/auth_controller.go)

go

CopyEdit

```go
package controllers

import (
    "github.com/dgrijalva/jwt-go"
    "myapp/models"
    "myapp/utils"
    "gorm.io/gorm"
    "github.com/gin-gonic/gin"
    "net/http"
    "time"
)

var jwtSecret = []byte("mysecretkey")

func GenerateToken(email string) (string, error) {
    token := jwt.NewWithClaims(jwt.SigningMethodHS256, jwt.MapClaims{
        "email": email,
        "exp":   time.Now().Add(time.Hour * 2).Unix(),
    })
```

```go
    return token.SignedString(jwtSecret)
}


func Login(c *gin.Context) {
    var input models.User
    var user models.User

    if err := c.ShouldBindJSON(&input); err != nil {
        c.JSON(http.StatusBadRequest, gin.H{"error": "Invalid input"})
        return
    }


    if err := db.Where("email = ?", input.Email).First(&user).Error; err != nil {
        c.JSON(http.StatusUnauthorized, gin.H{"error": "Invalid credentials"})
        return
    }


    if !utils.CheckPasswordHash(input.Password, user.Password) {
        c.JSON(http.StatusUnauthorized, gin.H{"error": "Invalid credentials"})
        return
    }
```

```go
    token, _ := GenerateToken(user.Email)

    c.JSON(http.StatusOK, gin.H{"token": token})

}
```

✔ Validates login credentials and returns a JWT token.

19.3.2 Implementing Task CRUD Operations

Task Model (models/task.go)

go

CopyEdit

```go
package models


import "gorm.io/gorm"


type Task struct {
    ID          uint   `gorm:"primaryKey"`
    UserID      uint   `json:"user_id"`
    Title       string `json:"title"`
    Description string `json:"description"`
    Status      string `json:"status"`
}
```

Middleware to Protect Routes (middleware/jwt_middleware.go)

go

CopyEdit

```go
package middleware

import (
    "github.com/dgrijalva/jwt-go"
    "github.com/gin-gonic/gin"
    "net/http"
    "strings"
)

var jwtSecret = []byte("mysecretkey")

func AuthMiddleware() gin.HandlerFunc {
    return func(c *gin.Context) {
        tokenString := c.GetHeader("Authorization")

        if tokenString == "" || !strings.HasPrefix(tokenString, "Bearer ") {
            c.JSON(http.StatusUnauthorized, gin.H{"error": "Unauthorized"})
            c.Abort()
            return
```

```
    }

    tokenString = tokenString[7:] // Remove "Bearer "

    token, err := jwt.Parse(tokenString, func(token *jwt.Token) (interface{},
error) {

        return jwtSecret, nil

    })


    if err != nil || !token.Valid {

        c.JSON(http.StatusUnauthorized, gin.H{"error": "Invalid token"})

        c.Abort()

        return

    }


    c.Next()

  }

}
```

✔ **Middleware ensures only authenticated users can access protected routes.**

Task Controller (controllers/task_controller.go)

go

CopyEdit

```go
package controllers

import (
    "myapp/models"
    "gorm.io/gorm"
    "github.com/gin-gonic/gin"
    "net/http"
)

var db *gorm.DB

func CreateTask(c *gin.Context) {
    var task models.Task
    if err := c.ShouldBindJSON(&task); err != nil {
        c.JSON(http.StatusBadRequest, gin.H{"error": "Invalid input"})
        return
    }

    db.Create(&task)
```

```go
c.JSON(http.StatusCreated, gin.H{"message": "Task created successfully"})
}


func GetTasks(c *gin.Context) {
    var tasks []models.Task
    db.Find(&tasks)
    c.JSON(http.StatusOK, tasks)
}
```

✔ Implements task creation and retrieval.

19.4 Testing and Debugging the Project

■ Unit Testing with testing Package

go

CopyEdit

```go
func TestHashPassword(t *testing.T) {
    password := "mysecurepassword"
    hash, _ := utils.HashPassword(password)

    if !utils.CheckPasswordHash(password, hash) {
        t.Errorf("Password hashing failed")
    }
}
```

■ Use Postman to test API routes

- Send a POST /api/auth/register request to register a user.
- Send a POST /api/auth/login request to get a JWT token.
- Send a GET /api/tasks request with Authorization: Bearer <token> header.

19.5 Deploying the Project Online

19.5.1 Deploying the Backend to Heroku

sh

CopyEdit

```
heroku login

heroku create go-task-app

git push heroku main
```

✔ Deploys the backend API to Heroku.

19.5.2 Deploying the Frontend to Vercel

1 Install Vercel CLI

sh

CopyEdit

```
npm install -g vercel
```

2 Deploy the frontend

sh

CopyEdit

vercel --prod

✔ Deploys the frontend to Vercel.

19.5.3 Deploying with Docker Compose

Deploy backend, frontend, and database using Docker:

sh

CopyEdit

docker-compose up -d

✔ Runs the full stack app with PostgreSQL in production.

✔ We implemented user authentication, task management, and middleware.
✔ We tested API endpoints with Postman and unit tests.
✔ **We deployed the application to Heroku (backend) and Vercel (frontend).
✔ The entire application runs smoothly using Docker.

Chapter 20: Becoming a Professional Go Developer

Go has become one of the **most in-demand programming languages** for modern software development, especially in **backend systems, cloud computing, DevOps, and microservices**. Becoming a **professional Go developer** requires a mix of **technical skills, real-world experience, and community engagement**.

This chapter explores **career paths with Go, open-source contributions, and strategies for getting involved in the Go community**.

20.1 Career Paths with Go (Backend, DevOps, Cloud, Microservices)

Go is widely used in various domains, and developers can specialize in different fields based on their interests.

20.1.1 Backend Development with Go

■ **Role:** Build and maintain APIs, web applications, and high-performance backend systems.
■ **Key Skills:**

- RESTful API development (Gin, Echo, Fiber)
- Database integration (PostgreSQL, MySQL, MongoDB)
- Authentication & security (JWT, OAuth)
- Performance optimization & profiling
  ■ **Common Tools & Frameworks:**
- **Gin** (Fast HTTP framework)
- **GORM** (ORM for databases)
- **Fiber** (Lightweight API framework)
- **Swagger** (API documentation)
  ■ **Job Titles:**
- **Backend Developer**
- **API Engineer**

- **Software Engineer (Go)**

Example Job Description

"Looking for a Go developer with experience in REST API development, PostgreSQL, and cloud deployment. Must be proficient in designing scalable microservices and implementing authentication with JWT."

20.1.2 DevOps & Site Reliability Engineering (SRE) with Go

■ **Role:** Automate infrastructure, manage CI/CD pipelines, and ensure system reliability.

■ **Key Skills:**

- Infrastructure as Code (Terraform, Pulumi)
- CI/CD automation (GitHub Actions, Jenkins)
- Logging and monitoring (Prometheus, Grafana)
- Container orchestration (Docker, Kubernetes)
  ■ **Common Tools & Frameworks:**
- **Docker** (Containerization)
- **Kubernetes** (Orchestration)
- **Prometheus** (Monitoring)
- **Terraform** (Infrastructure as Code)
  ■ **Job Titles:**
- **DevOps Engineer**
- **Site Reliability Engineer (SRE)**
- **Platform Engineer**

Example Job Description

"Hiring a DevOps Engineer with experience in Kubernetes, Terraform, and Go scripting. Must have expertise in building scalable cloud-native applications and managing observability with Prometheus."

20.1.3 Cloud Computing with Go

■ **Role:** Develop cloud-native applications and serverless architectures.
■ **Key Skills:**

- Cloud platforms (AWS, GCP, Azure)
- Serverless computing (AWS Lambda, Google Cloud Functions)
- API Gateway integration
- Distributed systems & microservices architecture
  ■ **Common Tools & Frameworks:**
- **AWS Lambda with Go**
- **Google Cloud Run**
- **NATS & gRPC** for communication
- **Message Queues (Kafka, RabbitMQ, SQS)**
  ■ **Job Titles:**
- **Cloud Engineer (Go)**
- **Serverless Developer**
- **Cloud Backend Engineer**

Example Job Description

"We are looking for a Go developer with expertise in AWS Lambda, DynamoDB, and API Gateway. Must have experience in serverless computing and event-driven architectures."

20.1.4 Microservices Architecture with Go

■ **Role:** Design and implement scalable, independent microservices.
■ **Key Skills:**

- Microservices design principles
- gRPC-based service communication
- API Gateway (Kong, NGINX, Envoy)
- Database per service pattern
  ■ **Common Tools & Frameworks:**
- **gRPC** (High-performance communication)
- **Kafka / RabbitMQ** (Event-driven architecture)
- **Istio / Linkerd** (Service mesh)

- **Consul / etcd** (Service discovery)
  - ■ **Job Titles:**
- **Microservices Engineer**
- **Backend Architect (Go)**
- **Distributed Systems Engineer**

Example Job Description

"Hiring a Go microservices engineer to design distributed architectures using gRPC, Kafka, and Kubernetes. Must have experience in API gateway configuration and event-driven communication."

20.2 Open Source Contribution and Community Involvement

Contributing to **open-source projects** helps developers build their reputation, improve skills, and **connect with industry experts**.

20.2.1 Benefits of Contributing to Open Source

■ **Gain Real-World Experience** – Work on real-world projects used by thousands.
■ **Build a Public Portfolio** – Your GitHub contributions showcase your expertise.
■ **Network with Professionals** – Get noticed by companies hiring Go developers.
■ **Learn Best Practices** – Improve coding, testing, and collaboration skills.

20.2.2 Finding Open-Source Projects to Contribute To

Popular Go open-source projects:

Project	Description	GitHub Link
Go	The Go language source code	github.com/golang/go
Gin	High-performance web framework	github.com/gin-gonic/gin
Cobra	CLI application framework	github.com/spf13/cobra
Prometheus	Monitoring system	github.com/prometheus/prometheus
GoReleaser	Automated binary releases	github.com/goreleaser/goreleaser

Finding Beginner-Friendly Issues

Many repositories label **"good first issue"** to help new contributors.

Run this search in GitHub:

pgsql
CopyEdit
```
is:issue is:open label:"good first issue" language:go
```

✔ **Shows beginner-friendly Go issues to work on.**

20.2.3 How to Contribute to Open Source

[1] **Find an issue:**

- Look for **documentation improvements, bug fixes, or feature requests.**
  [2] **Fork the repository:**

sh
CopyEdit
```
git clone https://github.com/your-username/gin.git
cd gin
```

3 Create a new branch:

sh
CopyEdit
```
git checkout -b fix-issue-123
```

4 Make your changes and commit:

sh
CopyEdit
```
git add .
git commit -m "Fixed issue #123"
```

5 Push your changes and create a Pull Request (PR):

sh
CopyEdit
```
git push origin fix-issue-123
```

6 Submit a Pull Request:

- Go to GitHub and open a **PR** with a clear description.

✔ **Congratulations! You've contributed to an open-source Go project.**

20.2.4 Engaging with the Go Community

Joining the **Go developer community** helps you stay updated and build connections.

- **Go Forums** – forum.golangbridge.org
- **Reddit** – r/golang
- **Slack Community** – Invite
- **Go Conferences** – GopherCon, DevOpsCon
- **Twitter / LinkedIn** – Follow **Go contributors and industry leaders.**

✔ **Backend, DevOps, Cloud, and Microservices are top career paths for Go developers.**
✔ **Open-source contributions improve your skills and increase job opportunities.**
✔ **Engage with the Go community to stay updated on best practices.**

🔴 **Next Steps:**

- **Pick a Go specialization** (Backend, DevOps, Cloud, Microservices).
- **Contribute to open-source projects** and grow your portfolio.
- **Engage in the Go community** to build your network

As you move from learning Go to mastering it professionally, it's important to keep expanding your knowledge. This chapter provides **recommendations for books, courses, and advanced topics** to help you deepen your Go expertise. We'll also explore **where to go next in your Golang journey**, including specialization paths, job search strategies, and community engagement.

20.3 Recommended Books, Courses, and Advanced Topics

20.3.1 Best Books for Go Developers

Reading books written by Go experts is a great way to **develop deep knowledge**. Here are some highly recommended books:

Book	Author	Description
The Go Programming Language	Alan A. A. Donovan, Brian W. Kernighan	Classic introduction to Go, covering fundamentals and best practices.
Concurrency in Go	Katherine Cox-Buday	Deep dive into Go's concurrency model with practical examples.
Go in Action	William Kennedy	Covers Go's internals and advanced features like Goroutines and Channels.
Hands-On Software Architecture with Golang	Jyotiswarup Raiturkar	Focuses on building scalable Go applications with microservices architecture.
Building Distributed Services with Go	Travis Jeffery	Covers techniques for building distributed systems with Go.

20.3.2 Best Go Courses and Tutorials

There are many great online courses to **solidify your understanding** of Go and learn industry best practices.

Course	Platform	Description
Go Fundamentals	Pluralsight	Beginner-friendly course covering Go syntax, functions, and structs.
Programming with Google Go	Coursera	Google-backed course covering Go basics and advanced topics.
Ultimate Go	Ardan Labs	High-quality training on Go performance and concurrency.
Building Web Applications with Go	Udemy	Teaches how to build REST APIs and web apps using Go.
Gophercises	Gophercises.com	Hands-on Go exercises covering practical programming challenges.

20.3.3 Advanced Go Topics to Explore

Once you're comfortable with Go basics, **exploring advanced topics** will help you stand out as a developer.

■ **Concurrency & Parallelism**

- **Goroutines** and **Channels**
- **Worker Pools** for handling high loads
- **Mutexes & WaitGroups** for synchronization

■ **Building Scalable Systems**

- **Microservices Architecture** with Go
- **Service Mesh (Istio, Linkerd)**
- **Event-Driven Architecture** with Kafka or RabbitMQ

■ **Cloud-Native Development**

- **Deploying Go Apps with Kubernetes**

- **Using AWS Lambda with Go**
- **Building Serverless Applications**

■ **Security in Go Applications**

- **JWT Authentication & OAuth2**
- **Best Practices for Secure APIs**
- **Handling SQL Injections & XSS Protection**

■ **High-Performance Go**

- **Profiling & Optimization with** pprof
- **Memory Management & Garbage Collection**
- **Load Testing with** hey **and** wrk

Mastering these areas will make you a **highly valuable Go developer** in the job market.

20.4 Where to Go Next in Your Golang Journey

After mastering the fundamentals and some advanced topics, **what's next?** Here's a roadmap to **becoming a professional Go developer**.

20.4.1 Choosing Your Specialization

The next step is to **choose an area of expertise** that aligns with your career goals.

Field	Specialization
Backend Development	Build high-performance APIs & web services.
DevOps & SRE	Automate cloud deployments with Go.
Cloud Engineering	Work with AWS, GCP, Kubernetes.
Microservices Architecture	Design scalable distributed systems.
Blockchain Development	Work on Go-based blockchains like Ethereum & Cosmos.
Game Development	Use Go for game engines & real-time processing.

Each specialization has **specific technologies** you'll need to master.

20.4.2 Landing a Job as a Go Developer

Here's how to transition from **learning Go to getting a professional job**:

■ **Build Projects & Showcase Work**

- Create a **GitHub portfolio** with real-world Go projects.
- Build **open-source contributions** to gain credibility.

■ **Get Certified (Optional, but Helpful)**

- **Google Go Developer Certification** (when available).
- **AWS Certified Developer (Go-focused cloud apps).**

■ **Apply for Go Jobs**

- **Best job boards for Go developers:**
  - golang.cafe
  - We Work Remotely
  - Hacker News Jobs
  - Stack Overflow Jobs
  - AngelList (for startups).

■ **Networking & Referrals**

- Join **Go communities** on Slack, Discord, and LinkedIn.
- Attend **Go meetups and GopherCon** to network with industry professionals.
- Follow Go developers on **Twitter and LinkedIn**.

20.4.3 Contributing to the Go Community

Becoming an active member of the **Go community** boosts your visibility and career prospects.

■ **Join Go Conferences & Meetups**

- **GopherCon (Global)** – The largest Go conference.
- **Go Developer Groups (Meetup.com)** – Local Go communities.
- **DevOpsCon & CloudNativeCon** – Covers cloud-native Go applications.

■ **Write Blog Posts & Tutorials**

- Share **your experience with Go** on Medium, Dev.to, or your personal blog.
- Publish **Go tips and tutorials** to help new developers.

■ **Become a Speaker**

- Apply to **speak at Go meetups or conferences**.
- Share your **Go projects and lessons learned**.

20.4.4 Building a Long-Term Career in Go

1. **Master the Language** – Keep improving by working on advanced Go projects.
2. **Stay Updated** – Follow Go release notes and new features.
3. **Engage with the Community** – Learn from experts and contribute.
4. **Level Up Your Skills** – Explore cloud computing, performance optimization, and distributed systems.
5. **Mentor Junior Developers** – Teaching others will reinforce your expertise.

✔ **Go offers diverse career paths in backend, DevOps, cloud, and microservices.**
✔ **Contributing to open source enhances your reputation and job prospects.**
✔ **Advanced Go topics like concurrency, cloud-native development, and security will set you apart.**
✔ **Networking, blogging, and public speaking accelerate your growth as a Go developer.**

● **Next Steps:**
➹ Choose a specialization and start working on **real-world Go projects**.
✊ Engage with the **Go community** and contribute to open source.
☛ Continue learning **advanced topics** to stay ahead in your career.

❗ **Remember, becoming a professional Go developer is a continuous journey – keep coding, keep learning, and keep growing!**

www.ingramcontent.com/pod-product-compliance
Lightning Source LLC
LaVergne TN
LVHW051427050326
832903LV00030BD/2961